COWARD A
CHEOLOGY OF
AGING

A SPECIAL ISSUE OF
PASTORAL PSYCHOLOGY

GUEST EDITED BY
SEWARD HILTNER

HUMAN SCIENCES PRESS
NEW YORK
1975

Standard Book Number: 87705-278-6
Library of Congress Catalog Card Number: 62-12633
Copyright 1975 by Human Sciences Press
Reprinted 1977

HUMAN SCIENCES PRESS, a subsidiary of
Behavioral Publications
72 Fifth Avenue
New York, New York 10011

Printed in the United States of America

CONTENTS

INTRODUCTION

It is a genuine pleasure to be able to present this special issue on aging to the readers of *Pastoral Psychology*. The essays were first presented as lectures at a Conference on the Theology of Aging sponsored by the National Retired Teachers Association and the American Association of Retired Persons during the spring of 1974. They consider in an ecumenical context the implications of theology for older persons and for the ways we think about the aging process.

The results of this conference contain some of the more thoughtful reflections on aging I have read. The writers locate the problem where it belongs—in the midst of our lives. They neither lead us to a wailing wall nor attempt to fill us with shame and guilt. Instead they ask us to think seriously about the aged and about aging, our own and that of the persons we serve.

As Editor, I would like to express appreciation to the NRTA and the AARP for permitting us to publish this material. In particular, I would like to thank Mr. William C. McMorran for his patient and persistent efforts to insure that no detail was overlooked in our efforts.

Finally, it is especially gratifying to have Seward Hiltner as Guest Editor of this issue. He helped plan the conference and then presided at the sessions. But, more than that, his history of association with *Pastoral Psychology*, the work he has done over twenty-five years to help form and sustain it, makes it "feel right" to have him lend an able hand.

Liston O. Mills, Th.D.
Vanderbilt Divinity School

FOREWORD

In 1973 the Church Relations Program, which is a service of the
National Retired Teachers Association and the American Association
of Retired Persons, decided to convene a high-level workshop of theologians to consider, in an ecumenical way, the implications of theology both for older people and for the process of aging. Such a workshop was held at St. Paul Theological Seminary, Kansas City, Missouri, on May 29-31, 1974. The participants in the conference were
primarily drawn from the Catholic, Protestant, and Jewish theological seminaries. The total group was small enough to engage in general
discussion following each address, and also to divide into smaller
groups for additional discussion.

The principal work of our staff in connection with the workshop
was done by W. Randolph Thornton, who was, at that time, Director
of the Church Relations Program. He was assisted by William C.
McMorran, then a theological intern. The staff also had valuable help
from the NRTA/AARP Executive Director, Bernard E. Nash. The
workshop was fortunate in securing the services of Seward Hiltner, of
Princeton Theological Seminary, not only to preside at the workshop
but also to help with the planning and, eventually, to serve as principal editor of the report.

Before the 1974 workshop, several conferences, both national and
regional, had been held to assist clergy and other church leaders in reflecting on their programs, actual or potential, in relation both to older people and to aging. It appeared, however, that the time had come
to stimulate more fundamental reflections at a theological level. It
was out of that sense of need that the 1974 workshop was conceived
and carried out.

It was a privilege and an honor for both of us to attend and participate fully in the 1974 workshop. We were impressed by the high
caliber of the addresses and discussion and pleased to be able to present the needs and concerns of many older adults.

Both NRTA and AARP are volunteer membership bodies, non-
profit and nonpartisan in character, committed to improving the quality of life for older Americans. The National Retired Teachers Asso-

ciation was founded more than a quarter of a century ago and the American Association of Retired Persons nearly twenty years ago. The founder of both organizations was Dr. Ethel Percy Andrus, who herself was greatly concerned about the spiritual aspects of aging.

While it is clearly recognized that the larger purpose of NRTA and AARP can be accomplished only if there is more widespread understanding of aging as well as of older people, both organizations develop programs to help older persons, programs for implementation on the local level. The resources of the Church Relations Program are therefore made available to all religious organizations, regardless of specific faith or denomination.

We believe that this report will be of interest to every thoughtful American. It is evidence that the theology of aging can be discussed by individuals coming from a wide variety of backgrounds and theological starting points. As a result, we believe that no serious discussion, either of principles or programs involving aging, should be held in the future that does not take the theological dimension into account.

Joseph A. Fitzgerald, President, 1972-1974
National Retired Teachers Association
NRTA/AARP National Headquarters
1909 K Street, N.W.
Washington, D.C. 20049

Douglas O. Woodruff, President, 1974-1976
American Association of Retired Persons
NRTA/AARP National Headquarters
1909 K Street, N.W.
Washington, D.C. 20049

Facts and Needs: Present and Future

Seward Hiltner, Ph.D.*
Princeton Theological Seminary

In my capacity as chairman of the workshop, I wrote a letter to all participants, summarizing my understanding of its purposes, which included the following:

> I have become even more convinced in recent years that the tendency to deny, evade, or otherwise fail to take seriously the confrontation of the aging process (before either person or group reach what is currently defined as older years) is either first or second on the list of "repressed" but vital concerns in our present culture. Now that sexual matters can be discussed and studied seriously, and even more recently death and dying have at least begun to be confronted, the avoiding of aging becomes both more evident and more lamentable.
>
> The one possible rival for the "most repressed important topic" that aging has is financial matters; but they would appear to be more consciously held in secret than actually repressed, as is the confrontation of aging. One incidental result of this repression is that there are, in an important sense, no experts on aging. Knowledge of transitions, successful or otherwise, from one stage of development to another, has increased greatly in the present century, especially through the first 35 or 40 years of life and, to a lesser extent, from late middle years into older years. But solid studies of the transition from young middle age to middle middle age and from middle middle age to older middle age are almost nonexistent. Even though the confrontation of aging ought not to begin only at 35 or so, it becomes crucial about then. And that is where our significant data are the sparest.
>
> Even though it will clearly be impossible to understand the problems of confronting aging (from various periods that are not old age), and doing something to improve the present evasion and denial patterns, without the work of persons from many professions and disciplines, it seems to me that a theology of aging (however defined in terms of content) has a unique opportunity and obligation. I am not thinking mainly in pragmatic or pro-

*Dr. Hiltner is Professor of Theology and Personality at Princeton Theological Seminary, Princeton, New Jersey 08540. He is an ordained minister of the United Presbyterian Church. Among his books are *Theological Dynamics* and *Preface to Pastoral Theology.*

grammatic terms, although what the churches say and do about "education for aging" may be practically important. I am more concerned with theology's rethinking of the whole question, remaining true to the essence of its heritage, but translating and, if need be, innovating concerning the meaning of aging in the most fundamental sense, in the light of the many new conditions of the modern world and the probability of more changes in such conditions in the years ahead.

As people now live longer, and soon will live longer yet, and more vigor may expected with the increasing life span, will aging seem to recede as something not to be confronted at all (until after 80, 90, or 100 years of living)? Is the sole, or even the main, theological question the confrontation of eventual mortality; or is it even more important to confront aging as a part of living itself? Is the wide use of the metaphor "maturing" ominous in that it stops when the apples are ripe? Is there a kind of "cryptic theology" in Erik Erikson's "generativity" applied to middle and older years; and if so, can this be brought out of vagueness especially by study and reflection at the theological level?

Some Current Facts and Figures

Between 1960 and 1970 the total population of the United States, according to official census figures, rose by about 24 million persons, from about 179 million to about 203 million (1). That represented, in the decade, an increase of 14%. During the same period, however, the proportionate increase in the population 65 years and over was greater than the general increase. During the decade the number of persons over 65 rose by 20% (about 4.5 million), and the number of those 75 and over increased by more than 37% (about 2 million). Less official figures than those of the census reports suggest that the proportion of people over 65 has continued to rise since 1970.

To understand the importance of the continuing increase in the population of older people, it is necessary also to keep in mind the trends relating to persons under age 65. The "baby boom" began during World War II and continued for a few years thereafter; it then went down slowly for a while and about ten years ago began a genuine decline that is continuing. There were nearly 16% fewer babies born in 1970 than in 1960. In contrast, the number of people from 15 to 25, products of the past baby boom, rose 48% during the 1960s. Among the other age groups (such as people in their 30's, 40's, and 50's), the changes during the 1960s were not great. Thus, the increases in the numbers and proportion of older people during the next 30 years will be due mainly to greater longevity and better health. But at about that time, the baby boom group will start to become older people; and for a while, the increase will be very great. At

the same time, both the number and proportion of new babies coming along will be decreasing.

Another way to look at the population is to compare the number
in what society now regards as the breadwinning ages with those who
are below or above that figure. In 1970 just a little over 52% of the
population was in the 20-to-65 age bracket. The over-65 plus under-
20 population was just short of 48%, with 38% being under 20 and
about 10% over 65. With the older group clearly increasing and the
younger group decreasing, it could be that matching the 20-to-65
group against the combination of over-65 and under-20 might remain
relatively stable for some years to come. But not less than 30 years
from now, the over-65 group may come close in actual size to the un-
der-20 group.

A few other facts about the over-65 group seem important enough
to note. In 1970 only 16% of the people over 65 were in the "work
force." Others were quite often (but it is not known how often) de-
prived of jobs against their wishes. Only 17% of couples 65 and over
had incomes of $10,000 or more; and only 13% of singles (especially
widows of course) had incomes of $5,000 or more. Only 5% of the
over-65's lived in institutions (that may not include all "nursing
homes," which have expanded rapidly since 1970), and a third either
lived alone or with persons who were not relatives. In the over-65
group there were four times as many widows as widowers. The sui-
cide rate in the United States for males, but not females, goes up with
age. At least as of 1970, if one wanted to live longer, he or she had
the best chance in Nebraska, Missouri, Kansas, Arkansas, and South
Dakota. Contrary to general assumptions, only about 20% of the over-
65's had "interference with mobility," except for the small proportion in institutions. The proportionate amount of dental care given
to over-65's was far less than for other groups in the population, despite the probability that they needed it at least as much if not more.

Trends Suggesting Theological Reflection

The trends to be mentioned here seem important occasions for
ethical and theological reflection, but they are far from being exhaus-
tive.

1. During the next quarter century there will be a steady increase
in the over-65 population so that by the year 2000 there are likely to
be about 30 million in this group. The percentage increase in numbers from now until then will not be very large, but at that time there

will come a kind of "over-65 boom." There are obvious questions about housing, health, and a living income for such persons. With the declining proportion of children and adolescents, society could solve those problems for older people. But does society value older people sufficiently to do what is needed?

2. Especially with the increase in vitality among older people, a larger proportion will be capable of doing work that can be contributory to society and also provide a needed sense of self-respect, even if the "jobs" are shifted from what they were in the middle years. At present society is lowering, rather than raising, the "retirement age," and offers fewer opportunities than before to older people for useful work in which they are interested. That trend defeats social productivity; much more important, it erodes the self-respect of many and, especially in men, accelerates the death rate for essentially nonmedical reasons. Can older people be both permitted and encouraged to "work" according to their wishes, strengths, and capacities?

3. We have, in effect, what might be called a possible "learning period" about aging in which the numbers of persons passing age 65 each year (for about 25 years) will grow but not greatly. That is the ideal situation in which to "teach" aging in years earlier than 65. After 25 or 30 years the number and proportion coming past 65 will greatly increase; so that if education is not well tested and in operation before that, the result could be chaos.

4. For the foreseeable future, older women will greatly outnumber older men. That situation could be somewhat altered: on the one side, the movement toward the liberation of women to do things not previously open to them might impede longevity for some; and on the other side, providing honest and useful inducements to personally rewarding and socially needed activity by men could increase male longevity. But such changes are likely to come slowly. Meanwhile, are there ethical and theological dimensions of the male-female imbalance after 65? Who may, or should, live with whom? Since we now know that sexual interest and capacity are still present in older years, does a new sex ethic need to be thought through (as it never has been in the past because the proportion of older people was quite small and it was assumed that sexual capacity stopped before older years)?

5. Our language confines "work" to money-earning, and its apparent opposite, "leisure," implies doing what you want and do not have to do. If, instead, "work" is the appropriate use of focused energy, and "leisure" is the enjoyable use of the time not spent with focused energy, then the need for reconsidering both work and leisure be-

comes imperative, first for older people but increasingly for the whole society, if education in aging is to be for all who should have it when they need it.

6. There are wide differentials in the potentialities open to older people according to the class and income structure, with radical departures from the average among those groups that are underprivileged or discriminated against in fact if not in theory. Some people may lose both self-respect and hope anywhere from their teens on. If honorable aging is to become something in which all may participate, then whatever can be done, at all ages, to eliminate discriminations moves toward that desirable end. Social action for aging is much broader than social justice for older people, and both are needed.

7. Perhaps the deepest question of all is whether the elements that dominate our society will continue their present ambivalent attitudes toward both aging and older people or whether the negative aspects of the present attitudes can be eliminated. This ambivalence has been fueled by many things—the nuclear family, population mobility, current residential architecture, the rising costs of Social Security, and others—but its roots lie much deeper and are probably very old, at least in Western societies. It may be at this point that theology's greatest responsibility lies.

Reference

1. Most of the figures were either given by or worked out on the basis of *General Population Characteristics: United States Summary* (Bureau of the Census, U.S. Department of Commerce, 1972).

Aging: Downward, Upward, or Forward?

Paul W. Pruyser, Ph.D.*
The Menninger Foundation

ABSTRACT: Life views are dominated by an iconic illusion that forces the span of life into a low–high–low sequence of stages. Aging is seen as loss, decline, a downhill course. But while there are losses in aging, there are also gains, and empirical observations show that many persons enjoy getting older. From a psychodynamic viewpoint the losses in aging, though painful, are made bearable by considerable gains that afford new pleasures. Aging's gains and losses are described, leading to the conclusion that the life course is neither upward nor downward, but a forward movement full of new discoveries.

While it is true that views on aging vary with culture and change with the times, nearly all Western views are similar in one respect, poetically expressed in Shakespeare's sonnet:

> When forty winters shall besiege thy brow
> And dig deep trenches in thy beauty's field,
> Thy youth's proud livery, so gazed on now,
> Will be a tatter'd weed, of small worth held. (1)

There it is: the overruling conviction that life has a peak, somewhere, with an upward and a downward slope on either side. It does not matter greatly whether the peak is at thirty, forty, or fifty years. Such differences may depend on the average expectable life span, the composition of the population pyramid, the epidemiology of illness, the economic system, and the educational and welfare policies of a society. The visual imagination sees a peak, flanked by valleys, one rising, one declining, in an aesthetically satisfying symmetry. Life views are shaped by a regnant Gestalt of low–high–low proportions,

---

*Dr. Pruyser is Henry March Pfeiffer Professor in the Department of Education of The Menninger Foundation, Topeka, Kansas 66601. He is an elder in the United Presbyterian Church. Among his books are *Dynamic Psychology of Religion* and *Between Belief and Unbelief.*

an iconic illusion that pre-sorts all perceptions of the life course into a triphasic sequence.

The Peak-Slope Illusion

There are infinite variations of this iconic illusion, each reinforcing the basic idea so strongly that we eventually lose sight of testing it. We take the illusion for reality, failing to check its veridicality, until a rare or unexpected occasion elicits some puzzlement. The variations are indeed so numerous that they can be classified. The *symmetrical* model of the peak flanked by two valleys comes through in the cresting ocean wave preceded by rise and succeeded by fall. It is inherent in graphic presentations of a great many statistical data that form the Gaussian curve, with its impressive middle section, tapered off evenly on either side. Its *literary* form is given in the "ages of man" of which Shakespeare's sonnet is only one example. The *linear* model presents the image of the arc of life describing a curve through space, again in a rise–peak–fall sequence. The *existential* version is a stretch of contingency, arched in the middle, suspended between the perplexing "thrownness" of birth and the appalling "pushed-outness" of death. The *journeyer's* model shows a crawling babe rising to become a walking, erect adult who in turn becomes a shuffling, cane-supported oldster. The *activity* model puts work in the middle, preceded by play, and followed by retirement, which may be just another word for play.

The *economic* model centers on the productive years, preceded by a vague stretch of consumerism that contains, happily, a teen-age market; and followed by the rentier's golden years that erode capital and produce no goods, but, happily, even so provide a market for nursing homes and retirement village builders. In *the arts*, our iconic illusion is reinforced by the triptychs of church altars with their major center panels and minor side wings; by the Laocoön group with its dominant, vigorous, high-rising center figure, and by the cascading structure of great churches and palaces whose major cupolas and spires are centered to draw one's gaze to a rise, peak, and fall pattern. Its *homeliest* form is probably the Victorian fireplace mantel arrangement whose centerpiece, the clock, is flanked by two ornamental vases that are kept completely dysfunctional. So much in the world proclaims a tripartite or triphasic pattern with a dominant center that we come to think of this pattern as a cosmic, ordained reality, and as a leitmotiv of life. This powerful iconic illusion thwarts us from seeing, or making, alternative patterns.

Facts, Valuations, and Experiencings

Yet there have been different visions. The Greeks prized youth and old age and seemed to find little to admire about the middle years. In some societies, the aged have such venerable status and benefits that aging is a positive goal of life and a desirable process. Systems of ancestor worship may put the aged on a pedestal. In some Eastern cultures, such as in the Sumatrese Menangkabau, the architecture of the house starts with a high-roofed, large center for the aging family founders, flanked on either side by ever lower-roofed ells in descending size for the family's offshoots. If these visions seem attractive today, it must be conceded that there have also been uglier views. Not so long ago, childhood and adolescence had almost no status of their own; adulthood was so dominant that children were namelessly absorbed into it as incomplete or defective adults. In some societies, older people have not only been denigrated, as they are by and large today, but were even sent into the wilderness to die. Enough to indicate that culture is a powerful determinant of attitudes toward aging and, hence, of feelings about selfhood at any age of life.

The impact of cultural factors on aging is so strong that it is foolish to belittle them as less real than the biology of aging. In principle, they may be more changeable than biological factors, but cultural change does not come easily. Though we are learning today from modern feminism that biology is destiny only in a large measure by a cultural fiat that makes it so, such fiats can in the meantime make or break lives. Just as feminism faces the enormous task of teasing out what is gender-specific and what is not so as to find starting points for change, and zones of flexibility or alternative life styles, studies of aging have to address the question of what is age-specific and what is not, and precisely in what sense anything is age-specific that appears so. That is no simple task. Beside scientific data-gathering the task requires existential inquiries and consciousness-raising, with keen alertness to the ideological consequences that follow from the dominant iconic illusion of aging.

It is very difficult to find even provisional agreement on what aging is. If aging is *growing*, in what sense does growing continue, stop, or change with the years? If aging is *coming of age*, time markers are introduced that set off one period of life from another for reasons of privilege and duty. If aging is *maturing*, the noun "maturity" introduces normative ideas about the course of the process denoted by the verb, elaborated by notions of "ripe," "over-ripe," and "rot" borrowed from horticulture, or by gastronomic notions of aging used in wine and cheese-making. If aging is *getting on in years*, we may think of judgment beginning to prevail over action, maybe of mellowing, perhaps of fatigue setting in; psychiatrists have reason to think of vulnerability to depression. If aging is *"seeing Abraham"* (metaphor for reaching the age of seventy), we celebrate a feat of endurance, with the afterthought that the landmark reached will also prove to be a turning point. And if aging is taken as the process meant to eventuate in *being aged,* it is largely seen as a foreboding of failing powers and eventual death.

With these variations in outlook and meaning, the so-called facts of aging have a rather dubious status. Many facts are functions of particular viewpoints, language games, measuring devices, disciplines, social observations, and personal experiences; few facts are wholly interdisciplinary or antecedent to any special perspective. Facts about aging tend to be quickly absorbed into images of man, supporting one or another ideological premise. And many facts are so minute and piecemeal that their import is unclear, since there is no way of assigning specific weight to them. For instance, autopsies have shown gross erosion of an entire brain hemisphere in older persons with exemplary physical and mental preservation, if not productivity and creativity, until their last days. How can we weigh such a fact against, say, the slowing of reaction times in reflexes over time?

But in the face of these difficulties of fact-finding and conceptualization, we should not allow ourselves to become nihilistic about understanding the aging process, let alone to deny its occurrence and its outstanding features. Denial, as a primitive defense against experiencing unpleasant realities, has already been raised to ideological proportions by too many philosophies, religions, and cults that seek to mitigate the pain of mortality by tinkering with its ontic status. There is, in the long run, no escape from experiencing that Augustine's famed three presents ("a present of things past, a present of things present, a present of things future") gradually assume different ratios in each person's life. Moreover, this is an entirely endogenous process, so basic that it serves as an ordering principle for the smaller facts and more ad hoc observations one can make about aging. Neither can one fail to observe or experience the waning of physical vigor and alacrity of mind as the years roll by. Death does lurk around the corner and can be held at bay for only so long. The vital balance quivers between the two forces of life and death, always precariously, and death has the edge in the long run, by the sheer weight of its inertia (2). Increasing awareness of this eventual inertia (the ponderousness [Latin "heaviness"] of death) and the feelings it engenders are everyone's lot in life and may be the primary definition of aging each person will arrive at for himself.

If this experience is basic and wholly endogenous, as I think it is, it becomes qualified by many special factors that originate in the particular body one has, the native and acquired idiosyncrasies of one's mind, the special situations by which one is shaped, and the vagaries of one's cultural learning. Body and mind have, moreover, some endogenous features of their own, which predetermine time sense; they also shoulder us with a temperamental inheritance that cannot be externalized. The experience of time, more precisely experiencing the *flow of our own time* in its backward and forward dimensions, is the subjective side of what philosophers call the contingency of being. But what we learn about that flow, what it does to us, the way we see it and react to it, depend heavily on other factors. Among these factors I attach great power to each person's exposure, at any time in his life, to examples of aging given by his seniors.

I think that personhood has much to do with two ranges of experience that are themselves interdependent: the experience of the flow of personal time and the experience of other people as love and hate objects. Children acquire their time frame from comparisons with the adults on whom they depend and with whom they identify themselves. Early life is full of verbal reminders of identification: "When you grow up. . . ," "When you will be as big as. . . ," "When you are as old as. . . ," occasionally interspersed with parental counter-identifications: "When I was a little boy, my mother used to. . . ." To the child, whatever the parent does or is seems desirable. This includes the parent's capacity for a long backward look in personal time, filled with memories. By identification with his parents, the child hungers for experience and rushes forward to close the gap between himself and his elders. But as Erikson has pointed out, parents need their children just as badly as the child needs parents (3). To the parents, much of what their children do or are seems desirable. They envy the child's long forward look filled with boundless expectations—a veritable ocean of possibilities, unlimited time for ventures, and second or third tries at things that did not succeed at once, and plenty of time for repair of mishaps, failures, or wrongdoings.

In the child's fantasy, the parent is immortal. To the parent's reality sense, the child is mortal but longevous. The parent's wish for his own immortality is reinforced by the child's fantasy about him. But it is checked by the present, which sees the grandparental generation's proven mortality shrinking the length of the personal future. We might say that aging already occurs when the reality principle overtakes the pleasure principle, when fantasies of immortality give way to realistic appreciations of mortality, for oneself and his loved ones. Or, as I suggested before, when the three aspects of time, as concretely experienced, become variable ratios, losing their original proportions. Awareness of these changes may come early or late in one's personal chronology—there is no fixed schedule for it. Some children grow up on an intimate footing with death; some very old persons find their own demise unthinkable. It is hard to say whether these shifts in awareness are aging or maturing—the choice depends on one's image of man.

Personhood, regarded from this angle, is an ongoing process of losses and gains, mourning and rejoicing—or, in technical terms, a process of cathexis, decathexis, and recathexis. We know quite a bit about the losses, and very little about the gains, because aging has so often been described, under the aegis of our iconic illusion, as a stepwise approach to decrepitude.

We should not deny or play down those losses, for coping with them is one of the taxing and energy-consuming features of aging, which itself may accelerate the aging process and set up spiral effects. In a way, aging is being put to a test of endurance: failure in coping with any specific loss undermines the aptness of one's response to the next loss, while success in coping with one loss may give one the vigor to face the next with bravery and skill.

Apart from the loss of loved ones through death, which does not necessarily increase numerically with advancing years, aging does entail personal setbacks experienced as loss. Among these, the following seem rather frequent and omnipresent, particularly for the average man or woman who has no wealth, no great talent, no especially favorable social position, no enduringly marketable skill, and little capacity or opportunity for sublimation.

Losses in Aging

If Simone de Beauvoir's recent lament is to be believed, and I am sure her picture is true for millions, aging entails a shocking loss of *personal dignity* (4). She perceives a societal conspiracy against the aged, particularly those who are forced into retirement, in which persons are put on the shelves, kicked upstairs if they are lucky, stripped of their raison d'être, and grossly exploited economically. In her view, social measures of care for the aged are mostly tokenist, if not a cruel mockery. Her picture is gloomy and contaminated by considerable political axe-grinding, and her statistics may be dubious, but these criticisms do not invalidate the correctness of her point of emphasis. The aged are subject to many indignities that are experienced as a frontal attack on their self-concept, their feeling of self-worth, and the maintenance mechanisms of self-regard. Whether these assaults on dignity are purely societal, or whether they are enhanced or per- petuated by the victims themselves through attitudes of self-fulfilling prophecy, makes little difference to the actuality of the experience, which is felt as a narcissistic blow. Perhaps these blows fall harder to- day, and are felt by more people than in former ages, due to the great increase in average life span expectancy from hygienic and nutritional improvements, medical "miracles," disaster control, and greater ease in living. If the average life expectancy is low, fewer people are ex- posed to the indignities of old age.

I think that *loss of work*, especially remunerative work, runs a close second in importance to loss of dignity, and may be intimately linked with it. If loving and working are pillars to mental health main- tenance, as Freud said, the reduction or stoppage of work undermines the very structure of personality. Work means so much and is so vital to personal integrity, as we know from studies of unemployed per- sons, that being placed outside the regular work force is a powerful factor in the dissolution of personality. The studies of Robert Coles (5), and particularly the recent book by Studs Terkel (6) describing the work of ordinary or low-income people, show that workers, by and large, tend to endow their jobs with a profound sense of voca- tion full of humanistic, religious, or ethical values that make them feel a significant part of a quasi-sacred scheme, even if they are by so- cial standards no more than cogs in the machine. Such attitudes to- ward work seem to capture some meanings of the theological concept of vocation or calling, in which work (of any sort) makes one a par- ticipant in creation and providence, giving each person a definite place and a significant role in a cosmic plan. Loss of work is in this sense loss of vocation, depriving a person of the concrete experience of values and meanings.

Work entails another factor of great importance to mental health (7). It provides a framework for reality testing: in fact, prescribes it by the structure and demands of the work situation. Work brings a person into forced contact with the nature of things and materials, with the resistance of matter, with the contours and definitions of ideas, and the nature of cause and effect relations, with sensory quali- ties, mass and force. This contact checks the unbridled fantasy, giving a counterweight to the wishes, longings, and impulses from the id, thereby providing a pivotal point for the ego's balancing tasks. Work draws us out of ourselves into the world; it forces us to deal with the actual outlines of reality, shoulders us with obligations, and harnesses our energies. Apart from the direct and indirect satisfactions it gives, work structures the flow of time for us into distinct periods for action and relaxation, work and play; it structures space in terms of home and shop. It structures thought and conversation by giving us opportunities to talk about our work while we are at home and to talk about home when we are at work. Loss of work demolishes this outer structuring device and forces us to impose arrangements on time and space and social intercourse that have to be created de novo by what inner structuring resources we have. Having to give up working, one's reality contact may become tenuous, with an automatic takeover by fantasies that are prone to lead to regression.

It seems to me that many, if not most, aging persons have to contend with a subtle sacrifice that may be described as *loss of independence*. This is a subtle thing because dependency and independence are relativistic notions; nevertheless, they are a powerful factor in life that comes to act·as a value orientation because development demands that we move in one direction from an original state of great dependency in childhood to one of independence in adulthood. This progression and its intensity are prescriptive; in our culture we are exhorted to be maximally independent. The ideal of maturity prescribes self-sufficiency, self-help, competence in managing one's own affairs, a display of unshakable strength in the face of adversity, the ability to seek and organize one's own pleasures and to ward off pain effectively, skill in seeking our own sources of contact and support, capacity for making friends, ability to earn one's own money, and strength to be a good spouse or parent or a satisfied single adult. We are trained to become competent managers of ourselves and our dependents. All these skills are signs of our acquired independence and proofs that we have left dependency behind us, that we have "made it."

If this is the maturational goal or ideal, how upsetting it is when events in the life cycle force us to surrender it, bit by bit. The upset is even worse when one incisive event, such as retirement, produces many losses at once. And how understandable that any new dependency is feared as an insult, evaluated as a regression, and experienced as loss of a once-prized achievement! Decline of income at retirement is felt as an acute loss, even when there are fewer mouths to feed. Decline of auditory acuity becomes a hearing loss, and the hearing aid an insult that comes to public notice. The bi- and tri-focal lenses show the world that we are losing our vision. Becoming dependent on gadgets and aids, pills and rest periods, memory props, and special

transportation arrangements, we feel we are losing our independence
and do not like it. For we have been trained to despise it, to loathe it
as a throwback to an utterly childish condition. Our image of personhood has failed to articulate the dependencies of the glorified independent adult.

Finally, aging is experienced by many people as a running out of
available time, as a *loss of time* in a special sense. Reality testing suggests that with more personal time behind one, there is less time ahead.
The future is no longer a virtually endless stretch. And there is still so
much to do, there are so many projects to start or finish, so many longings that should be fulfilled! In addition, there are persons who feel
that so many repairs must still be made of things done poorly in the
past, so many faults to be set straight, so much atonement to be un-
dertaken for previous transgressions. Small wonder that the feeling that
one is aging tends to promote a degree of agitation, restlessness, hurry,
or drivenness. This tendency is by no means confined to the late years;
it is recognized as an experience in the so-called mid-life crisis also.

In the retirement years, this sense of a loss of needed time becomes
oddly complicated by the fact that exemption from work also puts
much new chronological time at a person's disposal; he now has his
days free to spend as he wants to. But he may not know at all what
to do with this time; it is unstructured. Hence the conundrum: too
little time on the one hand, too much on the other hand; too little
for personal synthesis and further maturation, too much for dream-
ing, trifles, and busywork. Such situational ambiguity is likely to activate all kinds of personal ambivalence, which augments the agitation and makes the task of coping all the more strenuous.

To the description of these noteworthy experiences of loss I should
add a more basic meaning of loss to which these particular losses owe
much of their pain. The sense of aging to which I have called attention, which is an altered state of consciousness rather than a state of
physical wear and tear, derives its joys of gaining and its pains of losing from a primordial experiential model. That is the model of *object
relations*, the essence of which for our purposes is that selfhood is a
developmental and dynamic function of our relations to other persons, and vice versa. Other persons are our satisfiers, as we are theirs.
Important relations in life are reciprocal, not for ethical but for bio-
psychological reasons. Our nascent selves emerge from loyalties we
have toward others, and the love of others is co-determined by the
love we have of ourselves. Therefore, life is governed by some intriguing equations: to love is to be lovable, to be loved is to be loving, and
to be lovable is both to love and be loved.

Every gain in loving, being loved, and being lovable is satisfying and joyful; every loss is frustrating, saddening, and anger-provoking. Money, independence, success, competence, productivity, dignity, strength, fertility, a healthy and reliable body—all of these desirable things are taken as proofs of lovability when they come our way. They are also intertwined with our love for the significant persons in our lives who modelled them as virtues, who helped us achieve them, or who valued them greatly. Consequently, any loss that is felt as something being taken away from us by somebody (a person, group, government, fate, or god) precipitates a conviction of unlovability: we are no longer loved as we were before and can no longer love in return as before. Worse, the losses one sustains may not only be taken as signs of rejection but also become charged with irrational feelings of guilt and shame, which may turn them into punishment for transgressions or proofs of our disloyalties. Hence, to maintain adequate self-regard in the face of any loss—whether of limb, strength, fortune, faith, or dignity—is a taxing proposition.

We are now ready to see that the aged, particularly those of very advanced age, are prone to experiencing any or all of the aforementioned losses as *abandonment*. Being seen and heard in the marketplaces of life depends to a large extent on one's own initiative, drive, and agility; if any of these functions diminish, as they do in aging, through sensory and motor deficiencies and depletion of energy, one is simply less seen and heard, unless others make helpful efforts to give him a forum. Such extra efforts by others are frequently not made, be it from forgetfulness or malignant rejection. In either case, the aged person may well feel abandoned. This is a keen emotion that may powerfully re-enliven old childhood memories of abandonment and mourning; it may be experienced more intensely by knowing that one is approaching the ultimate abandonment of death. Small wonder that tearfulness is not uncommon in the very old—as in the very young.

Potential Gains in Aging

Up to this point I seem to have only reinforced the iconic illusion of a low–high–low sequential pattern. Much as I struggled to extricate myself from it, I have demonstrated how much I am still its captive. It is precisely at this juncture and after this confession that I ask the reader to consider the fact that many aging persons seem to take their successive losses rather well and do not succumb prematurely to the strains of aging. Why is this? Do they have exceptional coping skills, or does the aging process itself bestow gains and compensations for the losses it imposes?

Disregarding the special situation of the "happy few" who are highly endowed and whose knowledge and skill remain in demand and, therefore, do not actually retire, I would like to consider the masses who seem to age with a good deal of tranquility and considerable happiness. They must be making some psychic gains and experiencing some satisfactions along with the losses they sustain. What are these satisfactions, which, according to our basic assumption, must be proofs of their lovability, signs of being loved, and forms of the praxis of loving? This question is thrust upon us, in part, by the recent work of Ernest Hirsch, who finds that an amazingly large proportion of quite ordinary people over the age of sixty-five emphatically declare in a psychological interview that their later years are the happiest ones in their lives, albeit others find them quite miserable (8).

Maybe I should start by suggesting that one pleasure of aging consists in *the gradual discovery of some good and wholesome adult dependencies.* When the children have grown up, the parents begin to see how much they depend on their children's liveliness, attestations of love and goodwill, and their presence as objects of caring; sometimes this realization takes the painful form of the "empty nest" syndrome. Spouses, after having taken each other for granted, discover how much they need one another. By the time one has to face the necessity of planning for retirement, he discovers how much he depends on his regular work for daily satisfactions and mental equilibrium. From all such fragments of experience one begins to take another look at his former strivings for independence, to find some of it suspect. By hindsight, some of it was very demanding and overdone, and the promoted ideal of independence now proves to have been rather fictitious. With this realization, some relaxation sets in; one can acknowledge the healthiness of some dependencies and entertain the thought that some specific dependencies (e.g., on one's children, pension plans, friendships, recreation, simpler housing, mass transportation) are likely to increase with the years.

Along with the positive acceptance of some dependencies, satisfaction is had from *redefining one's own status.* Formerly defined by occupation, income, and social approval of one's demonstrated zeal for "making it"—all of which are external status definitions—the status of the person who knows that he is aging becomes increasingly defined by himself, in terms of his personal criteria. The achievement motive and the public applause for it give way to a search for idiosyncratic satisfactions; one begins to think of what he really likes to do, or what he will do the moment he retires. He may give up his house and roam the land in a trailer; he may start going back to college, not for career development but for his own edification. With the task of child-rearing done, couples may go on a second honeymoon and re-arrange their lives accordingly. One may start a new enterprise that turns a hobby into a second occupation in which work-pleasure gets the edge over profit orientation. One finds a new niche for himself that tallies with his native bent and preferences rather than with the dictates of upward mobility and pressures for conformity. Fateful as aging may be in many ways, it also gives new margins of independence for taking a greater hand in shaping one's own role and status.

The idea that aging can and should be gainful has long been held by Jung, whose concept of *individuation* stresses the significance of the second half of life (9). In a different conceptual framework, that emphasis is also present in Erikson's study of Gandhi (10), which documents the importance of the later stages of *identity formation.* Both notions imply that the latter half of life is not merely a decline but a period of new personality integration. For Jung, aging is opportunity for discovering one's own inner world as a worthy complement of, or alternative to, the external world to which one has been enslaved for so long, a chance to become aware of the neglected potentialities of the unconscious (the shadow), which have been kept dormant by the overexercise of functions demanded by the ideal of early adulthood. With a good deal of experience and many memories to look back on, one is in a position to take stock of oneself, to discover that much of what one took to be love was tinged with hate, that much of the self was thwarted by undue attention to the persona (the "masked" self of social expectation), or that keen strivings for action cut him off from the satisfactions of contemplation.

In Erikson's idea of *generativity*, the reorganization of personality takes a less introversive turn than in Jung's individuation, for it is attuned to two directions: the need of the mature person to be needed and the mature person's concern for guiding the next generations (11, 12). The latter is not solely one's immediate offspring but embraces, it is hoped, an ever wider circle of humanity with whom one can identify without pointed personal or parental narcissism. At any rate, aging loosens one from anxious concern with one's own dependents (the parental anxiety of "What is going to happen to my family if I die") to set one free for new and more flexible investments in all kinds of specimens of mankind at large, virtually without limit. One teaches the young, one stands up for his principles unabashedly, one befriends whom he wants to, one enjoys encounters with a great variety of people from all walks of life, one becomes less afraid of slurs of eccentricity.

Much of what I have thus far described makes room for some *relaxing of defenses*. With greater and more profound knowledge of the inevitable ambiguities of life and acceptance of irreducible ambivalence of one's own feelings, unpleasant realities can be faced with less denial, and negative affects or dubious propensities are no longer so prone to lead to reaction formation. Hypervigilance promoted by the rat race image of life can calm down to normal alertness. Some motives for defense begin to change, not the least of which is the reduction in drive level that many aging persons experience. Sexual attitudes and activities can become more relaxed—often with the effect of greater enjoyment and purer pleasure. Neuroticism tends to diminish with aging (albeit with intermittent moments of temporary exacerbation) and every diminution of a defense yields a quantum of energy that can now be put to freer use.

To put freed-up energies to use, older people often *seek or create work*, loading themselves up with tasks of all sorts that give personal satisfaction or are socially useful. This trend may be a defensive maneuver against the imminence of death ("There is so much yet to do that I cannot very well die"), but it is likely to be much more than that. As we saw before, work structures time and space, as well as personality. Much volunteer work, moreover, is of social or ethical value also. Some work produces gifts that convey love symbolically, to replace the erotic expressions of the past. How many grandparents have to their last days continued to make things for their children and grandchildren with unceasing effort and dedication?

Aging persons often report that they are *living in the present*, as distinct from their former rushing toward the future with feverish expectations and deep worries. They enjoy more because what they enjoy is now, in the present moment. The pleasures may be small and unspectacular, but they are real. If they feel they have a place in life, that place is here and now, and they are what they are, without much hiding or embellishment. I find this gain in aging nowhere better described than in Robert Coles's leisurely conversations with old people in New Mexico's mountain areas who enjoy the momentary sensory pleasures, muse a lot, accept much of what comes their way without the urge to intervene and change it, are thrilled by a short visit from a grandchild, and cherish the values to which they have been loyal most of their lives (13). If they are religious, the faith that sustained them in dark moments of the past, perhaps defensively, is now an enjoyable cosmology that beautifies and validates their present days. This observation stands in contrast to other cases, in which any religious idea or habit may be pursued with increased defensiveness as the years move on.

Speaking of faith or "philosophy of life," we must reckon with anyone's innermost subjective estimate of time left until death will overtake him. Most people entertain some fantasy about their approximate life span. Some know, intuitively or from family statistics, that they are hardy; others have been "nearly dying" most of their lives. In either case, advanced age grafts an inescapable reality factor upon these fantasies, The older one gets, the closer one moves into having to come to terms with dying. In his early fifties, Freud wrote in a letter to Jung: "Old age is not an empty delusion" (14). There are hard tasks to be done. Being very old means having to prepare oneself for death, pondering its meaning, or seeking a meaningful relation to its closeness. Faith, hope, love, and their permutations in all kinds of philosophies and religions are now put into the crucible— one becomes a kind of solitary alchemist doing his last "crucial" experiments.

This is the place for making a parenthetic but strategic observation. Given the minute age-specific groups into which the young have been subdivided in developmental psychology, it is remarkable how much tolerance we have for crudely lumping together "the aged" as though they formed one homogeneous mass. The category of "the aged" may span as many as four or five whole decades! Despite efforts at conceiving some subdivision, I am not sure that any compelling developmental distinctions have yet been made with a holistic tenor; most of them are of situational, fiscal, medical, or physiological orientation, or based on rather arbitrary chronological age brackets. We really do not yet know what the feasible distinctions are because we have been ideologically so resistant to investigating the process of aging.

I am also impressed by many aging persons' capacity to make *identifications* (or reidentifications) *with the idealism of youth* and their vicarious pleasure in the activism of youth. Skipping the intervening generation with its dedication to thought control and behavior shaping and its penchant for judging and disciplining, aging persons often feel attracted to youth and deal with young people in a relaxed way, tolerant of their foibles and positively charmed by their idealism and venturesomeness. Conversely, many young people feel attracted to the aged, finding them surprisingly congenial and avant-garde in comparison with the generation of their parents. The delight in grandchildren partakes of these qualities. In closeness to young children, the elderly can vicariously experience all over again the joys of perceiving and the thrills of discovery. The rediscovery of youth and its goodness amounts to a carefree caring that stands in contrast to the anxious (and more narcissistic) caring that prevailed during the years of parental responsibility.

There is a clue to one satisfaction of aging in the penchant of exceptionally accomplished persons, particularly scientists, for writing in their advanced years about their beliefs, sharing with the public their *personal credos*. I am impressed by those works that reveal the writer's metaphysical posture or religious faith, which strike the reader as "soft" in contrast to the hard-boiled rationality by which these men made their repute (15). Why do such books come so late in a person's career? To put it somewhat crassly: Why does a man have to be old before he can speak up about his personal values, beliefs, or faith? I do not think these questions are answered by pointing to the wealth of experience that must be accumulated over the years; I surmise rather that creative and productive persons in their prime often have to hide their deeper beliefs from their colleagues and the public, so as not to disturb their image and the conventions of their science or profession. As they grow older, there comes a point where they seize the freedom to distance themselves from the dogmas and techniques of their discipline, standing as persons above these. They no longer hesitate to speak personally; they have wrestled themselves free from a very sophisticated form of thought control to which they first willingly submitted for the sake of their careers and out of loyalty to their disciplines.

If this interpretation is correct, aging gives a *new freedom for revealing one's innermost thoughts*. I think this pertains to many ordinary people and is not confined to luminaries. However honest and open a person may have been before, aging gives him new candor for speaking without inhibitions. He reaps the satisfactions of a delayed honesty and a latter day openness that exceed everything he has been before. He has less fear of mockery and retaliation; he can now emotionally afford to show his heart in his reasoning. One might surmise that this freedom is in many, if not all, cases the fruit of the individuation process as described by Jung; a new personal synthesis is reached between the dialectical opposites of one's being. A former tightness and compartmentalization have fallen away. The freer spirit thus gained can also lead to an appropriate militancy in securing one's rights, or in doing battle for any oppressed part of humanity. I find its ferment present in the Gray Panthers, in Karl Menninger's activism for prison reform, in Einstein's sponsorship of worthy causes, and in the fabulous candor of I. F. Stone, the editor.

If these peculiar gains of aging are taken into account, without denying the losses that also occur, life seems no longer to fit the iconic illusion of the low–high–low sequence. A new image shapes up; it is as if someone put a bouquet of flowers in the right hand vase that stands on the Victorian mantelpiece. It has the power to distract our gaze from the dominance of the clock in the middle.

The botanical association is no whimsical happenstance. It has been made before, by no less than Goethe, in his eighties, in a memorable conversation with Eckermann:

> "From the letters which I have written in that period," said Goethe, "I can see quite clearly how one has in every age in life certain advantages and disadvantages in comparison with earlier or later years. For instance, in my forties I was about some things as clear and clever as I am today, and in many respects even better; but now in my eighties I have yet some advantages which I would not exchange for the ones I had then."
>
> "While you are saying this," [Eckermann] said, "I envisage the metamorphosis of plants, and I understand very well that one would not like to return from the period of bloom to the time of leafing, nor from the stage of seed and fruit to the time of blossoms."
>
> "Your simile," said Goethe, "catches my meaning perfectly. Take a well-lobed, mature leaf," he went on with a smile, "do you think it would like to go back from its freest unfolding into the oppressive closeness of the cotyledon?" (16)

References

1. William Shakespeare, *Sonnet No. 2.*
2. Karl Menninger, Martin Mayman, and Paul W. Pruyser, *The Vital Balance* (New York: Viking Press, 1963).
3. Erik H. Erikson, *Childhood and Society*, 2nd ed. (New York: W. W. Norton & Co., 1963), p. 266.
4. Simone de Beauvoir, *The Coming of Age*, trans. Patrick O'Brian (New York: G. P. Putnam's Sons, 1972).
5. Robert Coles, *Children of Crisis: A Study of Courage and Fear* (Boston: Little, Brown & Co., 1967); and, with Joan Erikson, *The Middle Americans: Proud and Uncertain* (Boston: Little, Brown & Co., 1971).
6. Studs Terkel, *Working: People Talk About What They Do All Day and How They Feel About What They Do* (New York: Pantheon Books, 1974).
7. Paul W. Pruyser, "Psychological Aspects of Working," *Reflection* 65 (March, 1968):1-6.
8. Ernest Hirsch, *A Spectrum of Lives* (Topeka: Menninger Foundation), unpublished manuscript.
9. Carl G. Jung, "The Psychology of the Unconscious," in *Two Essays in Analytical Psychology*, trans. R. F. C. Hull, Bollingen Series 20 (New York: Pantheon Press, 1953).
10. Erik H. Erikson, *Gandhi's Truth* (New York: W. W. Norton & Co., 1969).

11. Erikson, *Childhood and Society*, pp. 266-268, gives first description of generativity as an advanced stage in the "Eight Ages of Man." Passim in his subsequent works.
12. Don S. Browning, *Generative Man: Psychoanalytic Perspectives* (Philadelphia: Westminster Press, 1973).
13. Robert Coles, *The Old Ones of New Mexico* (Albuquerque: University of New Mexico Press, 1973).
14. Freud, in a letter to Jung of November 2, 1911. See *The Freud-Jung Letters*, ed. William McGuire, Bollingen Series 94 (Princeton: Princeton University Press, 1974), p. 453.
15. For example: Albert Einstein, *Out of My Later Years* (New York: Philosophical Library, 1950); Karl Menninger, *Whatever Became of Sin?* (New York: Hawthorn Books, 1973); Hans Selye, *Stress Without Distress* (Philadelphia: J. B. Lippincott & Co., 1974).
16. Johann P. Eckermann, *Gespräche mit Goethe*, vol. 2 (Leipzig: Phil. Reclam. Verlag, no date), pp. 96-97, discussion of April 12, 1829, translation by the author.

Eschatological Perspectives on Aging

David Tracy, S.T.D.*
University of Chicago Divinity School

ABSTRACT: Focus is on the reality of aging as the concrete expression of our common human experience of ourselves as temporal beings. The analysis appeals to resources from a philosophical interpretation of temporality and a Christian theological interpretation of the central symbols of eschatology. Both resources provide positive approaches and clarifications of that aging process. Three eschatological symbol systems are noted: the traditional (past-orientation); the prophetic (present-orientation) and the apocalyptic (future-orientation). Each is analyzed as articulating a distinct authentic possibility for a person or a culture involved in the aging process. Symbols help orientate us in a positive way toward the process of aging.

I am honored to be invited to provide some theological reflections on aging. Although I regret that I do not possess the kinds of expertise on the multidimensional question of aging to be found in this distinguished audience, I do hope that my own strictly theological reflections may be of aid to our collaborative enterprise. I do share the conviction that the question of aging is both one that should be central to contemporary reflection and one to which the Jewish and Christian theological traditions may be able to speak with some disclosive power. I would not presume to label my brief remarks here a Theology of Aging but rather some theological reflections that may prove of interest when that larger and more important collaborative task is attempted.

Accordingly, the article itself is divided into two principal sections: a first and relatively brief section will outline the nature of contemporary Christian theology as this paper shall employ that discipline. The second and major section will apply that understanding of theo-

---

*Dr. Tracy is Associate Professor of Theology at the University of Chicago Divinity School, 1025 East 58th Street, Chicago, Illinois 60637. He is a Roman Catholic priest. He has published *The Achievement of Bernard Lonergan* and *Blessed Rage for Order: New Pluralism in Theology.*

logical reflection to certains sets of Christian theological symbols that, so I shall suggest, may well have some disclosive power for an interpretation of the phenomenon of aging.

The Character of
Contemporary Christian Theological Reflection

In view of the radical pluralism present in contemporary theological reflection, it seems incumbent upon anyone employing that discipline to state as clearly as possible exactly what he or she means by "theology." I regret that here I must simply state my own meaning as distinct from defending it. Since I have tried to defend that meaning at length elsewhere and since the meaning is sufficiently representative of a wide variety of theologies not to be merely idiosyncratic (1), I trust that you will pardon these all too brief and introductory remarks on a complex subject. Summarily stated, I believe that a contemporary Christian theology is best described as philosophical reflection upon our common human experience and language and upon the Christian tradition (i.e., the significant texts, symbols, gestures, and personal witnesses of the Christian history). It should be noted that such an understanding of the task of Christian theology commits one to some not-universally-shared presuppositions. First, I hold that the theological task includes explicit reflection upon both the Christian tradition and upon our common experience. More technically formulated, our common experience is not merely an additional or supplementary *medium* for theological reflection but is a source on the same level with the Christian tradition itself.

Although I believe that this position is entirely defensible even on the grounds of the universalism implicit in the Christian tradition itself, for the moment I must simply state that belief in order to draw out its important consequences for our present discussion.

The most important of such consequences is also the second presupposition of this understanding of the task of Christian theology: that something like what Paul Tillich called a method of correlation must be developed and employed by contemporary Christian theologians. In short, if theological reflection demands both an analysis of our common experience and of the Christian tradition, then we must develop some critical way of correlating the results of those two distinct analyses. As is well known, Tillich suggested that this correlation consists in employing the central "answers" present in Christian revelation to respond to the central "questions" present in our cultural situation. We are all indebted to Tillich, I believe, not only for his brilliant defense of the need for a method of correlation but also for his specific analyses in the *Systematics* following from that correlation. However, there seems good reason to doubt whether Tillich's own formulation of the task of correlation really fulfills the ideal that he himself set forth. In fact, Tillich's understanding of the task of theology as involving "answers" from the message to "questions" from the situation does not actually correlate our experience and the Christian tradition but merely juxtaposes them by allowing the tradition to answer the questions from our experience.

In order to have a method of true correlation, we should critically compare both the questions and answers present in our experience (as the meaning of that experience is mediated by the kinds of reflection present in cultural analysis, human scientific analysis, and, at the final moment, philosophical analysis) with both the questions and answers present in the Christian tradition (as the meaning of that tradition is mediated by interpretation of the significant symbols, gestures, witnesses, and texts comprising Christian history). Such, at least, is my own understanding of the task of theological correlation. For our present task, I shall suggest that one major set of Christian symbols—the Christian doctrine or symbols of eschatology—bear intrinsic disclosive power for illuminating certain important dimensions of our common human experience of the process of aging: our sense of temporality and history.

I will conclude these introductory remarks on the character of Christian theological reflection, therefore, simply by stating that if indeed Christian theology is appropriately described as reflection upon both the meanings present in our common human experience and in the Christian tradition, then we may well turn to certain central symbols of the Christian tradition in order to see what questions and what answers may be offered in either our common human experience or in the Christian tradition. From there we may move specifically to certain central symbols of the Christian tradition in order to see what questions and what answers they may offer to the common human experience of aging, i.e., of experiencing our temporal selves in the process of history and nature. Since it seems clear that one question involved in the common human experience of aging is the question of how we may relate with authenticity to the temporality which defines that process and our very life as experiencing human beings, it makes eminent sense, I believe, to reflect anew upon the Christian doctrines of eschatology. For in those symbols, the Christian tradition articulates how the very process of temporality finds diverse but related authentic expressions. In reinvestigating the

Christian eschatological symbols in terms of this implicit temporal structure, then we may find whatever possible illuminative power these Christian meanings may disclose for that common human experience of radical temporality that occurs to anyone reflecting upon the process of aging itself.

Aging as the Concrete Experience of Time—Modes of Christian Temporality: The Prophetic, Traditional and Apocalyptic Experiences of Authentic Time

When one studies the Christian symbol system in the light of the modern understanding of temporality, it seems clear that, although any particular Christian doctrine or symbol can be interpreted in temporal terms, still the "eschatological" symbols are both the clearest and most powerful expression of the Christian understanding of human temporality. More exactly, although there seem solid reasons to believe that even the Christian doctrines or symbols of God and creation should be interpreted in temporal terms (2), still the eschatological symbols of the Old and New Testaments cast a uniquely illuminating light on the human experiences of temporality itself and thereby on the temporal sources of meaning for an individual or society or even a culture involved in the process of aging (3). In this section, therefore, I shall address myself to the question of our common experience of aging by raising the following questions.

First, is the process of temporality a positive or negative factor for our human existence as that existence can be understood in both our common human experience and in the Christian understanding of time and history? Second, how may the three modalities of time (past, present, and future) be said to constitute any given moment in the process of time itself? Third, what theological models may aid us in understanding how a particular modality of time (i.e., the past, the present, or the future) may find authentic dominance for a particular person, society, or culture at a particular period? If these reflections prove sound, then we can, I believe, provide a fully positive theological approach to the question of aging and an approach that explicates the diverse authentic attitudes available to us at different periods in our lives and at different moments in our societal and cultural experience.

Time as "Atomic Moments" or as Process

The entire analysis to follow can perhaps best be understood if one first recalls the familiar modern model for understanding time. It

seems clear that, for the modern as distinct from the classical Greek
or even the classical Christian mind, time is a fully positive notion.
We do not really aim to escape from time, history, process—or aging
as the concrete existential expression of these phenomena—in the
manner of the drive to an atemporal contemplation of the Greek tradition or the aworldly ascetical tradition of Greek and medieval Christianity (4). Rather the modern mind finds its principal, indeed con-
stitutive, locus of meaning in time, in process, in history. Accordingly, modern thinkers in a variety of disciplines have challenged not
only the classical disparagement of temporality as not fully real or
meaningful but also the classical—and still largely everyday—model for
understanding temporality. As Heidegger more forcefully than other
thinkers has shown, both the classical Greek philosophical views and,
more importantly, our everyday attitude and language manifest a profound misunderstanding of the phenomenon of human temporality
(5). For we are tempted to think—especially by our language and by
our commitment to clock-time—that temporality is really a series of
atomic moments—a series of "nows"—which "exist" literally for the
moment—for the now—then perish to yield to yet another "now."

Yet this understanding of the human experience of time as a series
of atomic moments—an understanding correctly described by Heidegger as "naive"—in fact tends to dominate our nonreflective attitudes
toward time. This domination of our language by clock-time and the
inherited Greek patterns of our culture distort our attempts to reflect
upon so central an existential expression of the very temporality of
our being as the phenomenon of aging. Is the very process of aging
not really a process at all but merely a series of atomic moments
whose final moment—like the midnight of those clocks we choose to
measure our hours—seems pointless? If there is no process of time,
then why not seek out escapes from temporality? Why not fear and
thereby prefer to ignore the very aging process that constitutes our
reality?

The intellectual and existential problem here seems clear: if we attempt to reflect upon the meaning of the phenomenon of aging by
means of this "everyday" model of temporal meaning as comprised
of a series of "atomic nows," then we are caught in an insoluble dilemma. That dilemma has two sides: first, this "everyday" model of
time can really provide no legitimate human meaning to the process
of aging but only to any given and really fictitious moment in the
process; second, this everyday model of time cannot illuminate how
either the past or the future can function meaningfully for any present moment since every moment is not merely distinguished but radically separated from prior and successive moments. With such an un-

derstanding of time, there is little wonder that Greek Christians were tempted to search—via the contemplative tradition—for some atemporal, indeed eternal, moment and were driven to reinterpret the temporal and historical categories and symbols of the Old and New Testaments in largely atemporal and ahistorical terms. If we do not attempt to remove this everyday model of time from our language and our reflections, then there is little hope that we ourselves or our pressure-ridden, our time-as-a-series-of-atomic-moments society can face squarely and with positive vision the aging process itself as one of the most concrete and most profound expressions of our authentically temporal selves. The liberation of our language and our experience go hand in hand; if we can break our ordinary notions of time, we may also be able to view our own aging as more than an occasionally glimpsed phenomenon, to be shunned at all costs. More exactly for our present more intellectual purposes, if we do not face and break this naive notion of time still operative in our everyday language and attitudes, then we cannot provide a meaningful understanding of the very process of aging itself or a meaningful understanding of how the past and the future relate to any present meaning.

I take it for granted that most modern persons accept the temporal and historical process as the central locus of their own self-understanding. Indeed, I believe that it is now clear that one of the permanent achievements of the modern consciousness is its fully positive interpretation of human temporality. That interpretation, moreover, is faithful not only to our common human experience of the process of temporality as interpreted by psychology and philosophy but also to the radically temporal and historical locus for religious meaning disclosed in the Old and New Testaments by modern exegesis and theology. From the viewpoint of the temporal meanings present in either our common human experience or specifically Christian symbols, therefore, we may clearly give a fully positive interpretation to the process of aging as the clearest existential expression of the process of temporality.

This positive interpretation seems clear and widely shared by most contemporary theologies as well as by most philosophies and human sciences. What is less clear, I believe, is the fact that the modern secular model for time as comprised of past-present-and-future meanings in any present moment may be further illuminated by the Jewish and Christian eschatological symbols. More exactly, when any one of us refers to a particular meaningful moment in his or her life, he or she presumably does not or should not mean simply a particular present

moment in a series of atomic moments. Rather he means (as, again,
stituted not only by the intensity of a new present experience but
also by the memory of relevant past experiences and the anticipation
or projection of future possibilities. In any given present experience,
moreover, the major source of meaningfulness may derive from either
the past (as in Proust's *Remembrance of Things Past* or the current
wave of nostalgia) or the present (as in a particularly ecstatic experience or presence with one's beloved) or the future (as in the anticipa-
tory power of hope present to revolutionaries in a despairing situation).

· The central point remains that *any* given moment can only be a
human experience if comprised of all three modalities of human time
—past, present, and future—even though the major source of meaning
for any given moment may come from the present, the past, or the
future. Now precisely this model of human temporality derived from
our common human experience of time clearly assures a positive interpretation of the process of aging itself and a positive affirmation
of the presence of both past moments (through memory) and future
moments (through anticipation) in any given present moment, and
thereby in the process as a whole. This model also frees the interpret-
er to focus upon the major source of meaning for any given moment
as either a past, a present, or a future meaning. As I suggested above
by means of some familiar examples (nostalgia, ecstasy, and hope) I
believe that this latter insight too can be found in our common human experience of time. However, I have also come to believe that
the same insight can be found in that diverse set of Jewish and Christian symbols we name eschatological symbols. How that might be the
case I shall now try to clarify.

Perhaps it would be helpful to summarize where this analysis has
taken us thus far. The argument has been that, from the viewpoint of
either our common human experience of time or the Judeo-Christian
understanding of temporal and historical meaning, a contemporary
theologian may in fact give a fully positive interpretation of the *process* itself of time and thereby of aging and a fully positive understanding of any given personal, cultural, or societal moment as constituted
by all three modalities of human temporality. Our question now becomes whether or not one of those modalities (past, present, or future) should be chosen as, in effect, the only authentic source of human temporal meaning. My suggested response is as follows: in both
our common human experience of authentic moments of time and in
our personal interpretations of the Jewish and Christian eschatological symbols, most of us, most of the time, are tempted to declare the

major source of meaning that we experience to be the *only* authentic source.

In our common experience, for example, many of those more advanced in the temporal process of aging may allow the past through memory to mediate most of their present meaning—whether that meaning be what the ancients called the wisdom of tradition or sometimes a merely diminished appetite for the present and the future (6). That the possibility of wisdom is an authentic attitude for some to take at certain later moments in the process of aging seems sound. Indeed other cultures—most notably the Chinese and, in Western society, the Italian—understand and revere the wisdom of age in a way that our own consumer-oriented and youth-oriented society often finds it difficult to comprehend. But by means of the present understanding of temporality we should be able to liberate our imaginations and our experience from the temptation to declare the aging process a cruel fate and the plight of the aged a seemingly cruel reminder of that fate. We may learn instead to respect the natural process of aging and the ever-fluctuating sources (past, present, and future) of our temporal meaning.

Modalities of Time in Christian Thought

In our attempts to interpret the Christian tradition, many of us are also tempted to announce that the real, the true, the authentic meaning of the Jewish and Christian scriptures on this question of the source of human meaning is, in fact, to be found only in those eschatological symbols that happen, curiously enough, to fit our own experience of authentic time (7). If we find that our common human meaning and thereby our religious meaning as well comes to us principally through our memory of past meanings, then we are encouraged to search out those expressions in the Jewish and Christian scriptures that speak to that past orientation. We may then decide that what may be called the traditional model for meaning is the key to all meaningful action (8). To be sure, there are warrants for this insistence in the scriptures themselves; in either the Priestly tradition of the Old Testament or the later "more Catholic" writings of the New Testament, one may, in fact, find what may be called a traditional mediation of meaning. More exactly, present meaning is mediated to a person or a community by that community's re-presentation (its memory) through word and sacrament of God's past, great actions (Exodus, or the new Exodus of Jesus the Christ) for that community. In short, the principal source of meaning for this "traditional" model is the past, which can and should be presented anew in the present and for the future.

The "traditional" mediation of temporal meaning, therefore, has warrant in the scriptures. The traditionalist is tempted to proclaim that only that source of meaning has real warrant. Happily, the other eschatological symbols of the scriptures disallow this insistence. Rather they speak not of one source of meaning but of at least three. For we also find in the scriptures, as we find in our common lives, expressions which indicate that for some the principal source of meaning is to be found in the present while for still others that principal source is to be found in the future. We may call the first insistence upon present meaning the "prophetic model" and the second the "apocalyptic model."

By the "prophetic model" here I mean simply the insistence that the locus of meaning for the authentic prophet is *present* action—repentance, conversion, social justice (9). That action is understood as the vocation that God's insistent demands place upon the prophet's present life by providing both a proper recollection of God's actions for Israel in the past and his promises for the future as the key to God's demands *now*. It seems clear that this prophetic type expresses the central understanding of the meaning of human temporality present in the major prophets of the Old Testament. As a type, the prophetic model is also found in the central present-oriented eschatological sense of temporality operative in the earliest synoptic and even the later Johannine and Pauline christologies, as interpreted, for example, by Rudolf Bultmann.

The shift to a future-orientation as the major source of *present* meaning can already be found in some of the prophets but does not represent the major present-centered emphasis of prophecy in spite of our everyday use of the futurist word "prophet." A future orientation only becomes a dominant type in the later books of the Old Testament period and in the intertestamental period when the fully future-oriented type of apocalyptic motifs begin to dominate the consciousness of the writers of these texts. As both Old Testament scholars and cultural analysts of the American experience in the sixties inform us, when prophecy fails, apocalyptic takes over. When neither the past tradition nor present prophetic reforms seem adequate to the crisis of a particular person or a particular culture, apocalyptic modes of thought begin to prevail. It may bear repetition to note that on the present model of *three* authentic modes of eschatological time, the apocalyptic and often revolutionary or future-oriented mode is a fully authentic possibility, however unnerving it may prove to be not only to the past-orientation of traditionalists but even to the present-orientation of reformists and prophets.

The fact remains that each one of us, as he experiences the process of aging of either himself or his culture, may recognize three possibilities at different moments in his own or his culture's life (10): first, the authenticity of respect for a tradition, whether that tradition be the Judeo-Christian tradition as with sacramental theologians or the tradition of Freudian morality as with Philip Rieff; second, the authenticity of prophetic demand for present reform, whether that present-orientation be the understanding of the need for constant decision for personal, societal, and cultural reform—indeed conversion—in every "now" represented by existentialist theologians like Sören Kierkegaard and Rudolf Bultmann or the somewhat more muted but still prophetic and reformist secular demands for present personal, societal, and cultural reform in the model for "generative man" developed by Erik Erikson and Don Browning; third and finally, the authenticity of the Utopian and often revolutionary future-orientation of authentic apocalyptic thought, whether that apocalyptic attitude be articulated in terms of the new Judeo-Christian theologies of hope and liberation or the cultural-apocalyptic vision articulated by Norman O. Brown. The latter insistence is important since apocalyptic thought is also clearly operative in the New Testament itself, not only in such obvious cases as the Book of Revelation but also, as Ernst Käsemann and Wolfhart Pannenberg remind us, at the heart of the milieu of the entire New Testament period.

The major reason for this brief description of the three major distinct types or models for temporality found in the scriptural writings is to suggest that a real pluralism of possibilities may be found in the Christian tradition as much as in our common personal, societal, and cultural experience. In our cultural experience each one of us is tempted to think that the major source of temporal meaning for himself (the past, present, or future) is the only authentic attitude to societal change (roughly the conservative, reformist, and radical) or even to the personal appropriation of the meaning of process of aging (roughly the too common conceptions of old age, maturity, and youth respectively). So too in our interpretation of the scriptural attitude toward the source of meaning in the process of time each one of us, on the basis of his own present experience of the temporal source of religious meaning, can find warrants in either the traditional, the prophetic, or the apocalyptic models of the Old and New Testament. The constant danger is to declare only our present meaning to be really meaningful. Indeed, how much contemporary theological debate is centered around this question! Is only the traditional (incarnational-sacramental) option an authentic Christian attitude toward time, as many Anglo-Catholics and Roman Catholic incarnational theologians seem to suggest? Is the prophetic attitude the only really authentic Christian option—as the existentialist theologians seem to suggest? Is the apocalyptic attitude alone the key—in Käsemann's famous phrase "the mother of all theologies"—as the various proponents of theologies and of the future seem to suggest?

Authenticity and the Eschatologies

My own position here is this: the major inauthenticity for any one of us is to declare that *only* and solely the traditional or the prophetic or the apocalyptic is the authentic option. If that option is taken—as it is all too often in both our interpretations of common human experience and our interpretations of Christian texts—then each group denies authentic time and thereby authentic life to the "other" group. Unfortunately, as the process of aging moves through our persons, our societies, and our cultures in its now traditional, now prophetic, now apocalyptic way, each one of us seems tempted not only to deny authenticity to the other possibilities ("Don't trust anyone over thirty") but also tends to harden and thereby distort one's own authentic grasp of meaning. That distortion finds its clearest expression in the constant temptation to literalize the symbols and myths of one's own position in order thereby to deny authenticity to the other. Such an unhappy fate seems to plague not only our present cultural history but Christian history as well. In the New Testament period itself, for example, the authentic mode of the "traditional" model of temporality represented in the New Testament phenomenon called "early Catholicism" can all too easily be literalized into that fateful phenomenon known as "extrinsicist ecclesiology"—"Extra ecclesiam nullus salus est." The authentic future-oriented mode of apocalyptic temporality can become the mere literalism of a mind-boggling and fundamentalist millenarianism. The authentic present-oriented mode of prophetic temporality can become merely a Gnosticism.

I have tried elsewhere—at length and with the kind of textual and historical evidence required—to suggest how all three modes of temporality have actually operated in certain signal periods of Christian history with both real authenticity and real inauthenticity. Consider, as one example, the Reformation period itself: there one finds the dominant mode of an authentically prophetic modality in Luther and Calvin; an authentically apocalyptic modality in the Left-Wing reformers, especially the Anabaptists; and an authentically traditional stance in the reforming decrees of the Council of Trent. Yet notice, too, how, with a few notable exceptions, the parties to that fateful historical discussion seemed genuinely unable to appreciate the other options as authentically Christian options. As a direct result of this failure, each major party also seemed unable to stop the hardening process of literalization of one's own insight into the Christian symbol system (11). The Tridentine traditionalist reform all too easily became merely the Counter-Reformation; the Lutheran religious and prophetic genius too quickly turned into the new Scholasticism of Lutheran orthodoxy; the Anabaptist apocalyptic vision too suddenly found a home in the mere literalism of a fundamentalist millenarianism. As a second theological example of this difficulty, consider the contemporary theological claims to the only authentic Christian view on the meaning of time in the present debate among the existentialist-prophetic theologians as opposed to both the traditional-incarnationalist theologians or the apocalyptic theologians of future hope! Such unhappy and misplaced disputes do not encourage one to believe that my present plea for diversity—i.e., for a recognition in the Scriptures of at least three distinct and related modes of authentic temporality—is as obvious as it may sound.

By all means, let us each argue the case for the relative adequacy of one mode of temporality in relationship to the other two. As I suspect this brief exposition of my own views has revealed, I do in fact hold that the present-emphasis of the prophetic mode is more appropriate to the meaning of the central texts of the Old and New Testament and more adequate to the meaning of our common human experience of temporality. I further admit that, from that theological "prophetic" point of view, I was heartened to find a similar kind of "relative adequacy" argument for a particular interpretation of our psychological experience in Don Browning's book, *Generative Man*, for, in present categories, Erik Erikson's "prophetic-or-present-oriented" model of "generative man" is more adequate to but not exclusive of our present experience than either Philip Rieff's more traditionally Freudian model of "psychological man" or Norman O. Brown's more apocalyptic countercultural model.

Indeed, the move to arguments of "relative adequacy" is precisely what seems needed here. But let us note that all such arguments only really show relative adequacy—as in Browning's work—in the context of a genuine recognition of diversity. Even if I choose one model to deal with temporality and aging as more relatively adequate there still remain other authentic options to merit respect and to teach further possibilities.

In summary, my suggestions in this section of reflection upon the Christian theological symbols of eschatology have taken the following logical form: from the viewpoints of both our common human experience and of the Christian tradition, we should approach the question of aging first by providing a fully positive theological account of the process of time and thereby of aging; second, by specifying how all three modes of time (past, present, and future) constitute any single present moment within the process; third, by analyzing in cultural and scriptural symbols alike how any single present moment, whether personal, societal, or cultural, may find its major source of meaning in diverse ways—sometimes from the past through memory (the traditional), sometimes from the present (the prophetic), and sometimes from the future (the apocalyptic). Such diversity, I believe, not only is more appropriate to the symbolic meanings present in the Hebrew and Christian Scriptures but also to our common human experience of shifts of attitude and thereby of sources of meaning in the temporal process itself.

If we can really learn to appreciate such diversity, then the process of aging need not take the all-too-frequent form of expressing exclusivist claims for the meaning of any particular moment in that process. Whether "young" or "middle-aged" or "old," we can learn to revere all three models of meaning (the traditional, prophetic, and apocalyptic) as each an authentic expression of our experience of time itself as at once the most natural and most human of our experiences. We can learn, perhaps, to appreciate how the natural process of aging can influence our own articulations of meaning in either a traditional, a prophetic, or an apocalyptic direction without having to deny the authentic humanity of other options or the authentic naturalness of our own ever-shifting experience of time and aging. No little problem with our present inability to reflect upon the process of aging seems to stem from our more radical inability to focus upon, to understand, and to respect the temporal self re-presented in and by that process in its full process-laden and diverse manifestations. Theology, one hopes, can aid in that reflection precisely insofar as it too is able to discover the temporal meaning laden in both our common cultural experience of aging and the great temporal symbols of Judaism and Christianity.

Aging and the Modalities of Time

If these reflections ring true, then one may also claim that, from the viewpoint of a contemporary Christian theology, the process of aging (as perhaps *the* concrete existential experience of temporality itself) may receive a fully positive Christian interpretation. Further, that interpretation may also find some illumination of its complex character by reflection upon the presence of all three modes of time in any moment in the process, and a recognition that, in any given moment in that process, a particular mode of temporality may dominate either authentically through a proper use of symbolic understanding or inauthentically through an improper literalization of that symbolic understanding. Does it not seem fair to conclude, therefore, that we can learn to respect, and indeed to revere, the natural process of aging as the most concrete expression of our union with nature and of our concretely unique—as human—temporal meaning?

If we learn that respect, then we may also learn to respect again— even to revere—but not romanticize, the diverse modes of authentic temporality and aging that each of us individually and, by analogy, our society and our culture may experience. Such an attitude of human and Christian reverence for all these authentic modes may free us to find our own most complete authenticity freed from the prison of consigning the mode of memory and tradition (concretely, too often the "aged") to the periphery of our respect in the manner too often associated with our own society's sometimes atemporal and consumerist attitudes as the latter are starkly and brilliantly analyzed in Simone de Beauvoir's *Coming of Age*. We may also free ourselves to revere but not to idolize our dreams for the future (concretely, too often the "youth") in such manner that we may challenge a strangely youth-oriented culture, which deprives both youth of its dreams and ourselves of our generative responsibilities. Perhaps, after all, the Christian tradition can help free us from that consumerist ideal of time as a series of atomic moments that tends to co-opt the young, imprison the mature, and forget the old. As such it may free us for a human recognition of our temporal meaningfulness and the natural reverence we owe ourselves and our fellows as we distinctly experience that temporality most concretely in the process of aging.

I am grateful for this opportunity to share with you some theological reflections on the process of aging. Those reflections have, perforce, been dominated by the properly theological focus on the general human-meaning factors (time and history), which may inform, perhaps even illuminate, the more specific studies of aging provided by the life sciences and the human sciences (12). Even theologically, however, my own remarks have been dominated by concerns that belong under the general rubric of history, not of nature. But perhaps my final plea for how an attitude of respect and reverence should be forthcoming from even this historical approach to temporality and aging may lead you to share my belief that a historically oriented theology, if allowed to pursue its investigations full sway, can eventuate in an attitude, an orientation of profound reverence for nature itself—including, indeed especially, that process of aging which represents at once our most concrete existential encounter with our own peculiarly human reality as historical and as temporal beings and our own clearest index to the profound and reverential harmony of our humanity with nature itself (13). If we may really learn to understand and reverence our own experience of aging in its historical-temporal and its natural dimensions, then we may also learn, I believe, to reverence as well those signal calls to authentic humanity, to which both the best of our contemporary interpretations or our common human experience of aging and the best of our contemporary Jewish and Christian theologies call us. What is fundamentally at stake in developing a Christian theology of aging, I believe, is but a reverence for ourselves as part of nature and a respect for the diversity of that temporal, aging self in such a manner that the integrity or dignity of every human being is affirmed without qualification. The Judeo-Christian symbol-system, I believe, can disclose precisely that reverence and illuminate that dignity. Theological reflection, therefore, may provide something like a horizon of meaningfulness, an orientation to the value of aging that may serve to clarify and strengthen the specific analysis found by the sciences.

References

1. The extensive defense may be found in my book *Blessed Rage for Order: New Pluralism in Theology* (New York: Seabury, 1975), especially chapters 2 and 3. Given the lecture format of this essay, notes will be kept to a minimum.
2. In the "process tradition" of modern Christian theology this is in fact the case. For a clear example, cf. Schubert M. Ogden, *The Reality of God* (New York: Harper & Row, 1966).
3. This remains the case given the fact that, whatever interpretation of the eschatological symbols of the Hebrew and Christian scriptures advanced as their full meaning ("realized eschatology," "proleptic eschatology," "futurist eschatology") still, by any account, these symbols clearly refer to temporality.
4. This is, of course, a generalization: faithful to the central tradition of patristic and medieval Christianity. In both periods more apocalyptic forms of Christianity tended to emphasize the more explicitly temporal character of eschatological symbols—as in the extreme case of Joachim of Fiore.
5. Cf. especially the classic texts in Martin Heidegger, *Being and Time* (London: S.C.M. Press, 1964).
6. The tradition of "wisdom" as articulated in Greek culture as the ability to order reality seems an especially valuable resource for understanding the possibilities and often actualities of the age-specific question of the "aged," preferably as the "wise."

7. It may be noted that there seems to exist a correlation between the general state of a culture (at its peak, in decline, in crisis, etc.) and the particular formulation of the temporal character of the eschatological symbols it chooses to emphasize. Analogously, a similar option seems often chosen at different moments in an individual's life.

8. "Tradition," it may be noted, bears here the fully positive meaning of a living *"traditio"* rather than simply those things handed down or repeated "traditia."

9. This interpretation of prophecy, although obviously influenced by such existentialist theological interpretations as Rudolf Bultmann's, seems wide enough to avoid the difficulties posed to a purely existentialist interpretation by such scholars as Von Rad and Pannenberg. Indeed, the debate on "prophecy" and "apocalyptic" provides further refinement but not, as far as I can see, a need to reject radically the general "ideal types" or "models" for both phenomena that I have developed here.

10. It should be emphasized that these categories are not intended as "age-specific" categories but as models for our humanity, which may, in principle, be found at any age. The correlation of these Christian theological models with the psychological-cultural models developed by Don Browning in *Generative Man* (Philadelphia: Westminster, 1973) is deliberate.

11. Perhaps the greatest signal danger for the treatment of Christian symbols is their literalizations, as epitomized in Reinhold Niebuhr's well-known adage, "Symbols should be taken seriously but not literally."

12. This is in harmony with my general position that philosophical and theological perspectives do not ordinarily provide specific solutions to specific questions but rather general value-orientations in the search for specific solutions. As such, they seem valuable conversation partners in the wider discussion.

13. A theological companion piece to this more historically oriented approach would be a theology of nature, as articulated, for example, in various Christian process theologies.

Jewish Values and Sociopsychological Perspectives on Aging

Robert L. Katz, D.H.L.*
Hebrew Union College—Jewish Institute of Religion

ABSTRACT: The Jewish approach to aging and the aged is constructive. If one no longer works, guilt is inappropriate. Old age may be a "sabbath" of human life. In our culture, older people are led to low self-esteem less by their age than by occupational and economic status. Hence fundamental social change is needed if there is to be dignity and quality in life for older people. Old age can become, as it should, the high point of the human career.

Despite vast medical progress we know relatively little about the phenomenon of aging. The term itself is imprecise and ambiguous. We do know some things about the processes of aging, one of these being that we begin to "age" while we are still in our late teens. We age at different rates; aging has different meanings for different people; to be aged may be a chronological variable because Picasso at ninety-plus had more vigor than some of us who would be loosely categorized as being of "middle age." Medical researchers only recently discovered that the arteries of young men can be "aged," while some people attain a "ripe old age" with cardiovascular systems resembling those associated with much younger people. Are we "aged" if we choose to retire at the age of forty-five or fifty, or are we "aged" when we first become eligible for social security? Do we become "aged" when we leave our own apartment and move into a residence complex where our fellow residents are classified as being "elderly"? There simply is no unequivocal meaning for the "aging" or "aged"; moreover, we cannot be sure when we are speaking in the language of physiology, psychology, economic status, athletic ability and physi-

*Dr. Katz is the Joseph and Helen Regenstein Professor of Religion, Ethics, and Human Relations at Hebrew Union College—Jewish Institute of Religion, 3101 Clifton Avenue, Cincinnati, Ohio 45220. He is a rabbi in the Central Conference of American Rabbis. Among his books is *Empathy*.

cal coordination, medicine and health status, political influence, familial role, or something else.

More than most of us realize, aging is a state of mind; we are what *we* think we are, the ways we perceive ourselves, and the ways we imagine our family and our community to perceive us. Aging is, at the very least, a relative term. A famous symphony conductor, now in his nineties, is still at work and now plans to build a new home in Venice. According to the calendar, he is indeed "old." But by what scientific, "objective" standards shall Leopold Stokowski be called old? If we speak of a so-called "life-span," he has comfortably exceeded the threescore and ten years of life cited in Psalm 90 but has some years to go before attaining the 120 years that Deuteronomy asserts Moses achieved. We conclude, then, that "aging" is an arbitrary nomenclature, a variable, subject to the widest interpretation. It is, therefore, important to consider the inputs both of religion and of science in trying to expand our grasp of the phenomenon of aging in our culture and in reaching for a system of values or attitudes that will be intelligent, realistic, and spiritually valid. Our statement will consider a number of variables, among them a variety of attitudes explicit and implicit in the tradition of Judaism.

Aging in Jewish Literature

According to one of the rabbinic homilies on the Bible, in early times it was not ordinarily the custom to take note of distinctions in age, even between father and son. When the distinction was introduced, it was for reasons of resolving an issue of status. Such was the case of Abraham and Isaac, according to the Rabbis (1).

> Until Abraham's time the young and the old were not distinguished from each other; consequently young people would jest with Abraham, taking him for their companion, whereas the old addressed Isaac in a manner becoming a man of years. This induced Abraham to pray to God for an outward token of dignity and honor for those advanced in years and the Lord, granting his wish, said, "Thou shalt be the first upon whose head the silver crown of old age shall rest" (2).

Aging here, as in so many Jewish sources, is presented as a valued status, one with privileges denied to others. Another source holds that old age is in itself not necessarily honorable. A man can be venerable without being old, while others live long without achieving character. For the rabbis, the ideal state was to attain both old age and honor.

Well known are the statements in the Bible mandating respect for
the aged. In Leviticus 19:32, we read "Thou shalt rise up before the
hoary head and honor the face of the old man." According to Prov-
erbs 16:31, "the hoary head is a crown of glory." Wisdom is associated
with the experience of being old, as in Job 12:12, "Wisdom is with
the aged, and understanding is the length of days." At the same time,
doubt is expressed about the inevitable accretion of wisdom with age.
In Psalm 119:10, the poet claims that he is wiser than the aged because he has excelled them in piety. In the Mishnah, a post-biblical
work (Ethics of the Fathers) note is taken of the fact that a new jar
can be full of old wine (wisdom) and an old one may not even contain new wine (4:20), but elsewhere in the context we are informed
that learning from the aged is like drinking old wine. A Talmudic
source goes so far as to maintain that the older scholars grow, the
greater their wisdom becomes (an opinion possibly reflecting the age
of the speaker).

Historically speaking, the Jewish community has tended to dem-
onstrate a care for the aged that is often taken to be exemplary. The
esteem in which the aged were held was expressed in tangible form
by a pattern of institutions caring for their needs. Even to this day,
Jews devote considerable time, energy, and resources to providing for
the aged so that Jewish solicitude is almost a stereotype. In the solidarity of the Jewish family, as it evolved almost to the present, we
may find an explanation for this care. Each member of the community felt responsible for the other and the aged were notably honored.
In the Jewish religious system, it was the elders who interpreted the
Torah, who transmitted it to successive generations, and who, in
terms of family structure and in the value-set of Judaism, command-
ed a loving authority and respect. Jewish community life had an integrity of its own, even as Jewish cultural and religious life main-
tained its continuity, adapting to a changing environment and yet re-
taining the "chain of tradition." In the Riesman typology of the personality types, the tradition-directed, as contrasted with the inner-
and other-directed, could be taken as a paradigm for the role of the
mature, if not the aged, in the Jewish family system (3). Since they
were the custodians of the tradition, they occupied a preferred status.
However, this reverence for the aged is not as intact or as consistent
in contemporary society. The Jewish family has accommodated to
rapid social change and has assimilated many values typical of the
other-directed society. The solidarity of the Jewish family today,
while still remarkable, is beginning to exhibit some signs of fragmen-
tation. Only recently investigators have found numbers of the Jewish

aged, abandoned and ignored in pockets of poverty in cities like New York and Miami. Sociological investigation indicates that some prevailing conceptions of Jewish family life must be updated and revised. But Jewish concern for the aged can, even today, hardly be dismissed as a stereotype. A deeply ingrained commitment continues to make this concern distinctive in a society that is conspicuously youth-oriented and that is directed by a peer culture largely cut loose from the past and from older, more stable patterns of family organization.

The Stages of Life

Since one of the tasks of this essay is to examine values and perspectives in Judaism rather than to review specific programs for the aged, we have been dealing primarily with religious literature. In general, we find a convergence between values found there and in the most enlightened secular writers today in the sociopsychological sciences. But before turning to some contemporary social thinkers, we need to take note of views in Jewish tradition of the aged and their place in the life cycle. While it is not at all certain what is meant precisely by the term "aged," most cultures, including the Jewish, conceptualize the stages of life. There is a sense of change of status as an individual ages chronologically; each stage has particular functions appropriate to the individual as he moves from one to the other. While the values respecting each stage have remained largely unchanged, there has been an awareness of change in the appropriateness of certain roles and responsibilities. One of the more familiar models in modern social science is of course the Eight Stages of Man as conceptualized by Erik H. Erikson, a psychoanalyst (4). Robert J. Havighurst, an educator, has also written of the "Developmental Task" (5). Such formulations were anticipated in Shakespeare and even earlier in the Bible and in Rabbinic Literature. The earliest reference to the Seven Ages of Man is by Hippocrates (357 B.C.).

The periodicity of human careers is most typically observed in the Book of Ecclesiastes: "for everything there is a season and a time for every matter under heaven, a time to be born and a time to die" (3:1). There is a painfully vivid description of the phenomenon of senility in the 12th chapter. The later years consist of "evil days" when the weak and the infirm have no pleasure in living. The images are dismal, evoking as they do the fragile and futile quality of those whose bodies are in acute decline. Nothing written since surpasses these few verses reflecting the physical deterioration of the senile. It is interesting that Maimonides, preeminent Jewish philosopher of the Middle

Ages, claimed that by following a proper hygiene, a set of morals, and a diet, no one need fall ill, and one can "achieve old age needing no doctor and enjoy perfect, uninterrupted health" (6). Ecclesiastes' description is still obviously pertinent because, even allowing for the successful achievement of old age, individuals, aging as they do at individual rates, ultimately will experience some fatal infirmity of body, though not necessarily the complete list so meticulously catalogued in the Bible.

In Judaism the most familiar description of the stages of life is found in the Mishnah, Ethics of the Fathers:

> At five years old (one is fit) for the Scripture, at ten years for the Mishnah, at thirteen for (the fulfilling of) the commandments, at fifteen for the Talmud, at eighteen for the bride-chamber, at twenty for pursuing (a calling), at thirty for authority, at forty for discernment, at fifty for counsel, at sixty to be an elder, at seventy for grey hairs, at eighty for special strength, at ninety for bowed back, and at a hundred a man is as one that has (already) passed away and ceased from the world. (7)

References to the Seven Ages of Man abound in post-biblical and rabbinic literature. One source holds that a man grown old is like an ape—if he is an ignoramus, that is. But if he is a learned man, he, like David, is a king. Another source describes man regressing into a pitiable state and becoming terrorized by his imminent death. Ultimately, the angel of death approaches him and asks him,

> "Dost thou recognize me?" to which he replies, "Indeed, I do; but wherefore dost thou come to me just this day?" "In order to take thee out of this world," says the angel, "for thy time has come to depart hence!" Immediately he commences to weep; and his cry pierces the world from one end to the other; addressing the angel, he exclaims, "Hast thou not already caused me to quit two worlds, to enter this world?" to which the angel finally replies: "And have I not already told thee, that against thy will thou art created, against thy will thou art born, against thy will thou livest, and against thy will thou must render account for thy actions before the Supreme King of Kings, blessed be He?" (8)

Man resists his destiny; life and death are thrust upon him but there is something for which he is responsible. He must defend his lifestyle, to use an overworked but still useful phrase, before God. That calls for some initiative and even creativity on the part of man. At this point the reader will associate along with me to the words of Erik Erikson, which resonate with the spirit of this image out of Jewish tradition, even though the Eriksonian perspective is anything but authoritarian or theological. In the Eighth Stage, Ego Integrity vs. De-

spair, the mature man, who works through to possess integrity, knows
that he must "defend the dignity of his own life . . . for him all human integrity stands or falls with the one style of integrity of which
he partakes" (9). These references to the stages of life and the age-
appropriate life tasks of man also suggest the concept of the monomyth, as developed by Joseph Campbell in his study of mystic themes
entitled *The Hero with a Thousand Faces* (10). Campbell interprets
the life cycle of man in the form of a "monomyth," which he feels
can be identified in major mythologies. The career of man involves
three phases: Separation, Initiation, and Return. The mature or aging
would fulfill the function of teaching and maintain the continuity of
man's traditions, after having achieved his own maturation and redis-
covered the basic wisdom of the human race. Every man, in Campbell's formulation, must accomplish the odyssey of the hero. He
writes: "A hero ventures forth from the world of the common day
into a region of supernatural wonder: fabulous forces are here en-
countered and a decisive victory is won: the hero comes back from
this mysterious adventure with the power to bestow boons on his fellow man"(11).

The Generations: Respect or Conflict

A recurring theme in all cultures is the accommodation of the generations to each other. Conflicts over power and privilege as between
the young and the old were as overt in classic times as they are now,
except that the alignment of forces has radically changed. Our society sees the aging as besieged by the young, now fighting a defensive
battle. The so-called "middle-aged" (like "aging," an ambiguous term),
while still in power, feel threatened by a youth-oriented society and
typically attempt to identify with the young and with their images of
what is humanly significant and precious.

We can better appreciate earlier vignettes of the war of the generations if we take note of some contemporary descriptions of the conflict. President John R. Silber of Boston University, who wrote so in-
sightfully about this issue in the *Center Magazine*, makes the association himself when he mentions the Fifth Commandment (12). If
mothers and fathers had been consistently honored, it would not
have been necessary for Moses to set down the commandment, "Hon-
or your father and your mother." Silber articulated the need of each
age group for the other and noted that when age groups are pitted
against each other, "we are murderous gangs—one intent on filicide,
the other on parricide" (13). He outlines his paradigm of the partnership of youth and age in these words:

If we reorder time to celebrate youth and age and the gradual metamorphosis from one to the other, if we regain our sense of time and value the present differences in the recognition that each of us plays all the parts in sequence, we shall see that there is no salvation for the young or the old at the expense of either. (14)

This thought is echoed in the statement by the psychiatrist, Seymour L. Halleck, who commented that:

A society which does not provide sufficient gratifications for the elderly will be an unhappy society for the young as well as the old. If the old are not gratified, nobody can accept the prospects of age with equanimity . . . for any society which cannot treat its elderly members decently is doomed to unremitting despair and chaos. (15)

Not the least critical element in the war of the generations is the raw competition for power and status. The elders, as Sebastian de Grazia wrote, never seem to die when young people wait and watch for their turn (16). The oedipus complex about which Freud has enlightened some three generations in this century distills the essence of generational conflict; even if the power and authority of the father in our culture are declining, Freud's paradigm is still useful in underscoring the recurring theme of competition, guilt, and hostility which reflect intrapsychic, interpersonal, and sociostructural variables.

References to social theorists would not be complete without including Margaret Mead, who discusses the generational encounter in her book *Culture and Commitment* (17). She notes that social and technological change make the wisdom of the elders little more than items of quaint archaeological interest. In the traditional cultures, the elder could invoke his own youth to understand the world of his children. Mead asserts that the generational gap in our culture is so firmly established that no communication would be possible on that basis. The prospects are not entirely desolate, however. The septuagenarian anthropologist allows a certain amount of space for the encounter of the young and the old. Where can they meet? In the joint enterprise, writes Dr. Mead, "The children, the young, must ask the questions we would never think to ask, but enough trust must be reestablished so that the elders will be permitted to work with them on the answers." Note the word "permitted." But age still has its validity: "father is still the man who has the skill and the strength to cut down the tree to build a different kind of house." And adults are still needed as models: "We must create new models for adults who can teach their children not what to learn, but how to learn and not what they should be committed to, but the value of commitment" (18).

It is because there are no guides—not just that the parents are no longer guides—that makes it necessary for young and old to find their way
in an uncharted land.

The generational conflict echoes in Judaism long after the procla-
mation of the Fifth Commandment. The sources identify the struggle
and, at the same time, hold out the prospect of a magnificent recon-
ciliation. Although our present conceptual apparatus is infinitely
more sophisticated and our grasp of social processes is documented
scientifically rather than theologically or poetically, we can still find
enlightenment in the truths about man and society evident in biblical
times. Familiar to many is the statement of the Psalmist (71:9) in
which the venerable writer calls out to his children: "Do not throw
me away in the time of old age, when my strength is failing me, do
not forsake me." The resolution of the generational conflict is an irreducible requirement for man's salvation in history; without it chaos
is inevitable. In Malachi we read, "Behold I will send you Elijah the
prophet before the great and terrible day of the Lord comes. And he
will turn the hearts of fathers to their children and the hearts of children to their fathers, lest I come and smite the land with a curse"
(4:5).

It is interesting to note, *en passant*, that the impact of this historic
passage is greatly diminished as reproduced in abbreviated form in
the Union Prayerbook (Reform) at the climactic conclusion of the
Day of Atonement services. Reference to the "great and terrible day
of the Lord" is deleted, leaving only the soft-spoken invitation to the
generations to turn to each other in love and become reconciled. The
potentialities for explosive conflict are seen dimly, if at all in the
prayers of reasonable and temperate moderns. But the potentialities
nevertheless exist. The resentments of the Grey Panthers come to
mind. The violence and repercussion of Kent State are most sugges-
tive of Malachi. The Talmud picks up this prophetic theme in discussing the portentous pre-Messianic days. "A sign of troubled times pre-
ceding the coming of the Messiah will be lack of courtesy and respect
shown by the young toward their elders" (19).

The following comment on a possibly historical episode reflects
the struggle for status between the young and the old. In this case,
the tradition puts the young down abruptly and absolutely.

> In the days of Hadrian, when enthusiastic young men advised the rebuild-
> ing of the Temple in Jerusalem, some wise men reminded them of the
> event that occurred in Rehoboam's time and said, "if young people advise
> you to build the Temple and old men say destroy it, give ear to the latter;

for the building of the young (done by) is destruction and the tearing down of the old (done by) is construction." (20)

Two visions of generational reconcilation need to be mentioned at this point, before turning to another theme. One is from the prophet Zechariah (8:4). It evokes the image not of violence in the street but of enchanting peace and beautiful symmetry of relationships. "Old men and women shall again sit in the streets of Jerusalem, each with staff in hand for every age. And the streets of the city shall be full of boys and girls playing in its streets." The following passage from Joel (2:28) seems congenial with the recommendation made by Margaret Mead, John R. Silber, and others that the generations form an effective partnership. The language of Joel is poetic and deeply moving.

> And it shall come to pass afterward,
> that I will pour out my spirit on all flesh;
> your sons and your daughters shall prophesy
> your old men shall dream dreams,
> and your young men shall see visions.

Aging and Social Class

We shall shortly consider the place of the aging in the classical theology of Judaism and note, in particular, the utopian, Messianic conception of the role of the aged.

Before that discussion, however, it will be useful to review some of the value orientations of American culture vis-à-vis the aging. What part do the aging have in a culture that still follows a Protestant work ethic, adheres to a philosophy of scarcity, submits to a life style of consumerism, and still esteems individual worth in terms of productivity, achievement, and upward social mobility? Moreover, what part do the aging have in a "temporary society," which has little regard for history and tradition and which is primed for rapid technological and social change? Even leisure time activity is something that is organized, managed, and carried out on schedule. The sense of stress is pervasive; the feeling of restless striving and incessant mobility is almost inescapable. What are the prospects for those who, like it or not, do have leisure, who may or may not be "productive," and who may not fit in with a consumer-oriented society? The temporary quality of life is especially uncongenial to those whose inclination for continued accommodation and change is no longer as strong.

It is important to recognize that one of the most important varia-

bles in the phenomenon of aging is class status. We can easily become
entrapped in the constraints of a middle-class orientation and find
ourselves generalizing on the basis of the social group with which we
are most familiar. This is typically a middle-class nation; even "lower" classes have a middle-class value system and internalize the perceptions of those normally considered more successful. When, for example, we speak of "disengagement" from the work force or use the
term "role exit" (coined by Dr. Zena Smith Blau), we are really think--
ing of middle-class people who radically change their life style when
they attain the age of retirement. They now feel called upon to re-
structure their lives and redefine their relationships.

These changes do not inhere in the reality of their chronological
age; they are functions of a changing socioeconomic position. Upper
class members whose income has been derived from ownership of
property or of stocks and bonds do not make a "role exit" when they
reach sixty-two, sixty-five, or seventy. They are not vulnerable to
many of the deprivations and dislocations of the middle-class aged.
For the rich, the advance of the years also has significance of course,
as it calls for accommodation to changes in the body and the loss of
a sense of physical well-being. But there is no less self-esteem. They
are not rejected by a social order that defers to power, wealth, and
acknowledged social status. Far from being abandoned by their family, their friends, and the community, they continue to command respect, hold positions of leadership on boards of institutions, and
maintain the quality of their life. Wealth does not command immortality, to be sure, but it normally discourages disrespect. So many of
the penalties age inflicts must therefore be viewed as deprivations of
social status rather than the absolute and irrevocable consequences of
growing old. Children and grandchildren of the powerful rich continue to defer to them. They pay visits to the patriarch and matriarch in
their winter and their summer homes. When such parents attain advanced age and require nursing care, they are not likely to be con-
signed to the warehouses for the aged and the infirm as is the fate of
the dependent and aged poor. They will not live out their years in
nursing homes, visited only occasionally and guiltily by their economically sufficient children. They do not live in fear of the erosion
of their pensions and Social Security income. They know their children will not set them adrift on an ice floe. The young, in fact, are
dependent on the patriarchs who still control the family fortunes.

The linkage of aging and social class cannot be emphasized too
strongly. Those of us who come from middle-class backgrounds wish
to excel our parents and rise above the status they have achieved. Our

parents encouraged us to move upward and beyond them. They take vicarious satisfaction in our achievements and take comfort during their retirement years that they have successful children who have "made" it. This satisfaction is an antidote to the pains and deprivations of their own diminished status. In the case of the rich and the privileged, elderly parents continue to be the models to be emulated; children are content to follow in their footsteps. The aged continue to symbolize success and their patronage is sought by community leaders, artists, and celebrities. Not for them is the state of near-panic of the man who faces retirement and the sudden reduction of income and loss of face. Most middle-aged people are unprepared for the transition into rolelessness. Their life style is to be linked to an uncertain income. But if you belong to a family of established wealth, you do not pass from one role to rolelessness with the elapse of time. You continue to practice conspicuous consumption because you have the means and you know that you belong to the privileged, happy few who have either won the race or have inherited the laurels of the battle. Society does not cease to pay homage to you because you have passed a certain age.

We need, therefore, to recognize the economic basis of our ideology of aging. It is not inevitable for men and women to fear the approach of retirement. The insecurity, loneliness, and loss of self-esteem that we assume to be normative to the aging process are in fact functions of a man-made social structure. In the words of Simone de Beauvoir: "Once we have understood what the state of the aged really is, we cannot satisfy ourselves with higher pensions, decent housing, and organized leisure. It is the whole system that is at issue and our claim cannot be otherwise than radical—change life itself" (21). The negative consequences of aging, de Beauvoir indicates, would be virtually nonexistent. Ultimately death would come but a person might expect to die without having suffered any degradation.

When a sociologist like Zena Smith Blau observes that there are two institutional structures, the nuclear family and the occupational system, that give "form and meaning to adult existence in modern times," she speaks out of the middle-class bias (22). De Beauvoir's perspective, which is that of a generalist rather than that of a one-dimensional sociologist, provides a broader vista of possibilities for enhancing the human condition.

New terms often move us to a new consciousness about familiar realities. Our grasp of the process and meaning of aging can be informed by the term "elective years," which was suggested by a newly retired doctor, George A. Perera, writing in *The New York Times* on

March 6, 1974. He rejects retirement, although he is giving up his occupational role. It is the continuity of one's life that is important:

> Please let me grow old and call me old, even aged if need be. I do not want
> life to be divided into categories with sharp lines between them. I want no
> disguise or falsification of my advancing years. Life, from its inception un-
> til its cessation, is a continuity. I want to be part of it and savor it all, even
> the inevitability of death.

Old age can be a time when, liberated from the pressures and hang-
ups of a youth-oriented society that is driven and harassed by guilt
and insecurity, we relish the meaning of life.

Older people should be able to act, live, and take pleasure without
having to make every act a moral act. Philip Slater wisely observes
that young people are locked into a thought system that they cannot
shake off, even though they think of themselves as radical critics of
the status quo. Slater writes: "The puritanism of youth displays itself
in an inability to act without ideological justification. Every act becomes a moral act" (23). If the young cannot slow down the pace
and relax without guilt, the aged, by contrast, ought to be able to sa-
vor life quietly and leisurely. They can cultivate the art of living and
count the blessings of each day, all the more precious because it is
lived more fully. It is the aged who can "live for the day" rather than
the young, who rush about transforming the future. De Beauvoir calls
our attention to the very moving words Claudel write in his *Journal*,
at the age of eighty: "Some sigh for yesterday! Some for tomorrow!
But you must reach old age before you can understand the meaning,
the splendid, absolute, unchallengeable, irreplaceable meaning of the
word today!" (24).

Because we still adhere to what Slater calls the "ice-floe approach"
to the aged, we are unable to envision the possibilities of secure,
meaningful, and even joyous life styles for the aged. We associate status with productivity. We believe everyone must work as long as possible, moonlight if necessary, achieve, and strive. We continue to believe, blindly and tenaciously, that we live in a culture of scarcity and
must therefore fight each other for our share of the limited stock of
supplies available at any given time. Once again the class variable must
be kept in mind. Only the middle and lower classes live in the oppres-
sive ambiance of the scarcity culture. Families that have ascribed status and enjoy financial security live in an economy of abundance.
Their destiny is not competition and upward mobility; it is living in
the style to which they have been accustomed and maintaining stable
and comfortable patterns. They do not struggle to survive or to tran-

scend the standard of living of the parental family. The rich, even if
they are idle, are, of course, not without existential anxieties. But
they do escape the deprivations of loss of status.

It is not only conceivable but may already be within the grasp of
our generation to move from scarcity to abundance. We have sufficient resources and technological capability to provide the good life
for all our citizens, regardless of their class or their age grouping. But
the belief that the goods of life are in short supply is so strong that
we move slowly, if at all, towards a society organized to guarantee
total security for all age groups. It is the aged who are the victims,
along with members of minority groups, of a society that resists radical social change. We can console ourselves with the knowledge that
the means for a good life for all are close at hand. But for the aging
of the middle and lower classes, such consolation is too little and too
late. If anything, their dissatisfaction and impatience grow all the
greater, knowing, as they do, that the means are at hand for an economy of abundance in which they might live with dignity and without
loss of self-esteem. For the present, the social ideology of the aging
calls for a fairer share of the goods, privileges, and benefits of the social system as now organized. This viewpoint generates pressure on
government and competition with other groups. For the aged, time
has run out for a program of social reconstruction. The emergency is
now; it will do them little or no good to wait. For the country as a
whole, however, it is essential to develop a new ideology of the aging
and renew our commitment to a society of justice and equality. Ultimate fulfillment for the aging can come only in that day of prophetic
peace and righteousness envisioned by Micah (4:3): "They shall sit
every man under his vine and under his fig tree, and none shall make
them afraid."

Aging and the "Sabbath" of Man's Life

In concluding this paper, we return to the theme of Judaism and
the aging. The prophetic words of Micah remind us of the main thrust
in the Jewish tradition toward a belief that the universe is not resistant to the fulfillment of man's hope. There is no reason for any individual or group to compromise their expectation for a life lived to
the fullest in a setting of the greatest possible security.

Often religious establishments deny what Marcuse calls "the explosive element" in the teachings they represent (25). Keeping company
with scientists who examine and define the status quo and distance
themselves from issues of direction and control, we, in institutional

religion, tend, in the words of Marcuse, to "accustom men to a good conscience in the face of suffering and guilt" (26). In reflecting on the religious approach to the situation of the aging in our culture, we might recall the impressive responsibility Marcuse allocates to us: "Where religion still preserves the uncompromised aspirations for peace and happiness, its 'illusions' still have a higher truth value than science which works for their elimination" (27).

In the Jewish view, adumbrated in Scripture and developed more fully in post-biblical Judaism, man is not only encouraged but obliged to hope for salvation. In the vision of the end of days—a time of peace and love—the aged, too, will attain happiness and enjoy the highest esteem, for they represent man in his state of highest self-fulfillment as a child of God.

Life becomes an unending Sabbath for the individual attaining the years of maturity; it persists for him until the day of his death. Nothing captures the essence of the theology of aging in Judaism as does the concept of aging as the Sabbath of the soul with its rich possibilities for self-realization (28).

It is important to note that work does not have the same meaning in Judaism as in other religious traditions and therefore ceasing to work and observing the Sabbath has a different rationale and ethic. The distinction between labor during the work week and creative activity on the Sabbath—or in one's so-called retirement years—is vital to the understanding that the Jewish sources contribute to the issue of aging. Work, in the ethos of the Western, middle-class culture, amounts to no less than the primary source of an individual's self-image, his identity, and his self-esteem. A person is valued because he produces; he occupies a status in the economy. Rolelessness or disengagement from the work force is, therefore, dreaded because the individual now suffers from anomie and knows that his community considers him at best an ornament of sentimental interest and, at worst, as a throwaway, used-up object.

In the Messianic thought of Judaism (not in the contemporary Jewish community, regrettably), the individual who attains old age is not only not degraded but is honored. The aged can now address themselves to high purposes such as the study of God's word and the purification and refinement of the soul of man. Nothing is lost if man does not have to work; he may still enjoy the Sabbath. As a matter of fact, for him each day is now a Sabbath. The passage in Genesis (3:17) presenting man as toiling life-long to earn his bread has not been taken in Judaism as establishing work as anything like an absolute value. Labor does not serve the function of compensating or atoning for guilt. Necessary as work may be, it is not, as Rabbi Lamm wrote, "an autonomous virtue" (29). It may be true that it is "natural" for man to work—in Genesis 2:15 he is enjoined to till and keep the Garden of Eden—but it is not the necessary condition for salvation.

As the Sabbath is the climax of creation, so the time of maturity represents the highest point of man's development. In the "Sabbath days" of his old age, man has the opportunity not to rest, although he may do that, but to "refresh himself." In the passage in Exodus 31:17 God rests and is refreshed. What God does is paradigmatic for man. Resting, in that passage, signifies cessation from work; being refreshed refers to activity that is creative and active and yields a sense of renewal and inspiration. Ceasing to work does not mean becoming idle or aimless. With leisure comes the opportunity for another kind of activity, the goal of which is the cultivation of one's soul and its potentialities.

What we find in Judaism, therefore, is a magnificent defense of leisure. In the language of the rabbis, Judaism sanctifies time. You do not "kill" time or "pass" it to fill the void left by retirement. You use it for study, prayer, or contemplation. And if these finer arts do not engage your attention, you fulfill yourself in other ways without feeling inner guilt and without experiencing rejection by the community.

Maimonides wrote a description of the Messianic time for those readers inclined toward philosophy and religious study. But his words suggest a perspective and a dimension that can be profoundly stimulating to those of us today who seek new values for the aging and who protest the "envy and competition" that presently divide the generations. What, then, are we to do in our leisure and our old age so that we may enjoy self-esteem and possess a sense of salvation? Maimonides wrote:

> The Sages and the Prophets did not hope for the coming of the Messiah in order that they might rule over the world, or have dominion over the other nations, or that they might be glorified by other peoples, or in order to eat and drink—but that they be free to engage in the study of Torah and its wisdom, without anyone to oppress them or distract them, so that they might thereby deserve the life of eternity.
>
> In that time (of Messiah) there will be neither famine nor war, neither envy nor competition. Goodness will be available in great abundance, precious things as commonplace as dust. *And the business of the entire world will* be only to know God. . . . (30)

Very few of our aged are endowed with sufficient worldly goods to be able to escape the fate of being stateless, roleless, and virtually homeless. Often they are abandoned by friends and sometimes, by family. They need sensitive pastoral care. They need, too, to sit in a place of dignity with none to make them afraid and with many who will come to them for blessing.

References

1. Cf. *Jewish Encyclopedia*, s.v. "Age, Old," for original sources.
2. Ibid.
3. Cf. David Riesman, *The Lonely Crowd* (New Haven: Yale University Press, 1950).
4. Erik H. Erikson, *Childhood and Society* (New York: W. W. Norton & Co., 1950), pp. 219-34.
5. Robert J. Havighurst, *Human Development and Education* (New York: Longmans Green, 1953).
6. Hilchoth Deot.
7. Chapter 5, 21.
8. *Jewish Encyclopedia*, s.v. "Ages of Man in Jewish Literature, The Seven."
9. Erikson, *Childhood and Society*.
10. Joseph Campbell, *The Hero with a Thousand Faces* (New York: Meridian Books, 1956), p. 30.
11. Ibid.
12. John R. Silber, "The Pollution of Time," *The Center Magazine* 4, no. 5 (September-October 1971).
13. Ibid.
14. Ibid.
15. Seymour L. Halleck, "What Adults Have Against Children," *The Enquirer Magazine*, Cincinnati, February 6, 1972, p. 35, reprinted from the *I B M Think Magazine*, November-December 1970.
16. Sebastian de Grazia, *Of Time, Work, and Leisure* (New York: Twentieth Century Fund, 1962), p. 153.
17. Margaret Mead, *Culture and Commitment* (New York: Natural History Press, 1970).
18. Ibid.
19. Sotah 49b.
20. Toseft. Ab. Zarah 1:19.
21. Simone de Beauvoir, *The Coming of Age*, trans. Patrick O'Brian (New York: Warner Publications, 1973), p. 807.
22. Zena Smith Blau, *Old Age in a Changing Society* (New York: Watts, 1973).
23. Philip Slater, *The Pursuit of Loneliness: American Culture at the Breaking Point* (Boston: Beacon Press, 1970), p. 80.
24. De Beauvoir, *Coming of Age*, p. 666.
25. Herbert Marcuse, *Eros and Civilization* (New York: Vintage Books, 1955), p. 66.
26. Ibid.
27. Ibid.
28. Cf. the essay by Rabbi Norman Lamm on "Ethics and Leisure" in his *Faith and Doubt* (New York: Ktav Publishing Company, 1971), pp. 187-209.
29. Ibid.
30. Maimonides, Mishnah Torah, Hilchot, Melachim, 12.4 ff.

Preface to a Practical Theology of Aging

Don S. Browning, Ph.D.*
University of Chicago Divinity School

ABSTRACT: To address theologically the issue of aging is to confront the problems of practical theology. The problems of aging give us an opportunity to begin afresh our reflections upon the nature of practical theology. A practical theology of aging must take experience seriously. It must use phenomenological description and empirical analysis to open up the surface and the depth dimensions of experience. But then the results of these labors must be correlated with a hermeneutics of Christian symbols. When the results of these endeavors are pooled, the key to meaningful aging emerges as learning to "care" for oneself, one's future, and the future of the race.

The task that has been assigned to me is a challenging one. I am to reflect on Erik Erikson's concept of generativity, discussed at length in my book *Generative Man*, and attempt to develop a theology of aging with Erikson's contributions in mind. Such an assignment throws me head on into issues in theological method of the most subtle kind. In fact, it goes even further and requires me to attempt an exercise in practical theology. To address such a topic—with all of its sensitive personal and social implications—is to obligate one to go beyond foundational theology and enter into specific policy discussions pertaining to the way our society should order itself to accommodate the transitions involved in aging.

To address the possibility of a theology of aging within the boundaries of this essay forces me to limit my remarks to a few programmatic notes about method for a theology of aging. We should recognize that the contemporary theological task must proceed in a pluralistic religiocultural context; for this reason theology must ask what

*Dr. Browning is Associate Professor of Religion and Psychological Studies at the University of Chicago Divinity School, 1025 East 58th Street, Chicago, Illinois 60637. He is an ordained minister of the Christian Church. Among his books are *Generative Man* and *The Atonement and Psychotherapy.*

it can contribute to and how it can evaluate other contemporary perspectives on aging and, further, upon what grounds it can assert that
what it would contribute is true or valuable.

This last remark exposes my theological stance. It is my conviction
that theology in the modern world must be philosophical reflection
upon the truth and relevance of specific religious traditions. It is the
task of theology to develop rationally defensible articulations of the
meaning of human life that answer man's religious needs for wholistic
visions and orienting frameworks for the guidance of everyday practical activities. Theology must be rational, especially in the context of
modern highly differentiated societies. We must interpret rationally
our orienting faiths in order actually to articulate the basis of their
truth and value and to relate them concretely as a source of guidance
to the various arenas of our complex modern existence. Theology, as
I will be using the word, refers to the philosophy of religion of a particular religious tradition—the Judeo-Christian tradition of the West.

What are the sources of theology when understood in this way? If
theology is to be philosophically convincing, it must draw its truth
from an *interpretation* and *correlation* of two sources—common experience *and* central themes in the Judeo-Christian tradition. To base
theology on the central witnesses of this tradition alone is to leave
theology to the vagueness of confessional circularity whereby theological assertions are tested by neither their adequacy to experience
nor their comparability to other competing interpretations and answers. The intelligibility of the central themes of the Judeo-Christian
tradition is enhanced if they can be correlated with pervasive meanings embedded in our everyday common experience.

Such a procedure requires some method of interpreting the basic
meanings implicit in common experience. It is my judgment that two
procedures are required. First, a phenomenological analysis of our
pre-reflective experience of being-in-the-world—along the lines of
methods practiced by Merleau-Ponty, Sartre, the early Heidegger, and
the early Ricoeur—offers an effective method for both describing our
basic sense of freedom and grasping basic meanings resident in experience prior to the inevitable interpretations we place on them at later
stages of reflection. But I am convinced, as are Paul Ricoeur, Merleau-
Ponty, and others, that our pre-reflective experience of the world is
opaque and that our direct descriptions of this experience are necessarily ambiguous unless they are themselves correlated with scientific
explanations. Merleau-Ponty argues this point of view when pointing
out the difficulties of subordinating pure phenomenology to empirical psychology (1). He writes: "The essences we may discover, when

we force ourselves to think about lived experience, are not, in Husserl's terms, 'exact essences,' capable of an univocal determination. They are, rather, 'morphological essences,' which are inexact by nature" (2). Paul Ricoeur argues very much the same point when he insists that phenomenological description of "living experience" should be supplemented by "objective knowledge" derived from the empirical sciences (3). But because he starts with phenomenology, Ricoeur reverses the point of view of the empirical sciences. Consciousness no longer becomes a "symptom" of the physical body or mechanical psychological states; rather, what we learn about ourselves objectively at the level of our bodily processes or psychological mechanisms becomes "symptomatic" and "diagnostic" of our prereflective experience, clarifying that experience at a level to which phenomenological description cannot reach (4).

We have only the space and time to list quickly the remaining steps that must be taken in developing a practical theology of aging. First, the meanings uncovered in our phenomenological and diagnostic reading of common experience must be correlated with the central motifs of the Judeo-Christian tradition. The motifs must be uncovered by careful historical and hermeneutical analysis. The actual correlation itself comes about by an imaginative grasp of *structurally analogous* dimensions of the two levels of meaning—those from common experience and those from the central motifs of tradition (5). Those dimensions of meaning from the two sources that enjoy analogical congruence to one another gain philosophical prominence and become candidates for the next two steps in our efforts to develop a practical theology of aging.

The next step must involve a basically metaphysical enterprise. These structurally analogous meanings from the sources of common experience and tradition must be submitted to metaphysical examination and amplification. The question must be asked: in the context of what theory of the nature of events and their interrelations can these meanings be considered as true of man and his world? It is only when this question is answered that the statements of theology (and this includes practical theology) can be considered true.

But to show that a set of theological statements can be true is not exactly the same as showing that they have value for man in his existential situation (6). In order to take this final step—which is the step from foundational theology to practical theology—the "answers" yielded by our earlier procedures must be applied to a careful analysis of man's existential *and* sociocultural situation. In addition, attention at this point must be paid to the question as to whether "an-

swers" from theology "fit" this situation better or worse than other
competing answers, ideologies, and faiths.

Obviously, within the confines of this brief paper, I can do nothing more than partially illustrate what these procedures might mean
for developing a theology of aging. In addition, we will have to slight
the very important task of reviewing and assessing proposed social
legislation designed to improve the situation of the aging. Instead, I
will address the primary task of theology, which is to provide orienting interpretations of life and human destiny that constitute the truth
and value frameworks governing the development of both social policy and strategems of individual intervention and care.

A Phenomenological Description of Aging

From the broadest possible perspective, aging refers to the simple
process of moving from the beginning to the end of life. But common usage in our everyday language provides a more precise prelimi-
nary point of entry to a working definition of aging. In common usage, the word "aging" refers primarily to perceivable evidence of
physical and mental decline. Hence, we tend not to talk about a person aging until certain external manifestations appear (wrinkles in
the face, less energy, forgetfulness) even though the subtle physiological processes that lead to these changes have been silently working
their subversion long before they become externally visible. The idea
of aging holds within it an implicit concept of the life cycle—the idea
that human life has the rhythm of expansion and decline. Common
usage also suggests that there is no simple correlation between physiological and social-psychological decline. This is why we hesitate to
refer to some middle-aged people as aging; physiologically certain external signs of decline may be visible, but socially and psychological-
ly their lives appear to be expanding. Therefore, common usage suggests that although physiological aging may influence sociological and
psychological aging they are not synonymous.

This first effort to arrive at a definition of aging has taught us that
the concept implies a view of life as a cycle with a rhythm of expansion and decline. Furthermore, the concept of aging emerges as a temporal concept, referring to a temporal transition from the past to the
present and the future, or better from beginning, middle, to the end.

Let us now locate ourselves somewhere in the middle of the cycle
of life in an effort to discern some abiding structures of meaning
about aging that common experience yields. I will use both phenomenological description and scientific explanation in the fashion of

Paul Ricoeur and Merleau-Ponty as discussed above. My work—tentative as it must be for this paper—suggests the following formula. Aging comes to us as an *external* and foreign impingement and evokes *concern.* Our response to this imposition of aging can be a *free* one, but our freedom necessarily must take the limited forms of either *consent* or *denial, care* or *self-preoccupation.*

Looking at aging phenomenologically from the perspective of the person in his or her late thirties or early forties, one is impressed with how little our direct experience of ourselves in our world tells us about aging. From a phenomenological perspective, *knowledge of aging comes to us primarily as a witness mediated through the external world.* Knowledge of our aging comes to us first through the reflection in the mirror, the gestures of others that communicate that we have changed, and the analogical application to ourselves of the knowledge that since our neighbors are growing older so most probably are we as well. Of course, there is direct testimony of aging in our immediate experience, but the signs are ambiguous. For instance, we cannot traverse time and space as well as we once were able to do. Nor can we work as long and as hard. We cannot run as far and as fast as was once the case. But the signs are ambiguous. Is it because we are out of shape and out of practice, or is it because we are physically declining? It is only because we see around us older people and know that it has been the universal experience of all humans that they some day become old that we know how to interpret these first ambiguous signs of physical decline. Also, scientific knowledge serves as further external, objective "diagnostic evidence" that this slight loss of vitality that I think I experience is "real" (7). It is partially because knowledge of our aging comes to us primarily as something external to our immediate experience of ourselves that awareness of aging is so easily denied. Aging seems to come to us from the outside as the future possibility of indefinite forms of decline and eventual death (8).

This aging that I discover happening to me evokes *concern.* Aging is a mediated part of my experience; I first see it happening to others and then to myself through the gestures of others. But the concern that aging evokes is directly a part of my experience. *I am concerned.* But the content of this concern is difficult to uncover. Due to aging I am concerned that the scale of my life will be *narrowed* and that eventually it will *end.* But my concern is a diffuse concern. I am anxious over the possibility of suffering a reduction of the boundaries of the self and an eventual loss of myself. But I am also concerned about my world. Because to lose myself is to lose my world and I have always thought of myself in relation to a world of people, family institutions, projects, and values. Aging evokes within me a concern for both myself and my world. This concern is an anxiety, but it is also a positive concern to preserve both myself and my world.

Finally, phenomenological description of my pre-reflective awareness of aging reveals that I can respond to aging with *freedom*, but that my freedom is a limited freedom. I am free to *deny* or *refuse* the fact that I am aging. This is easy to do because growing old is an ambiguous and largely mediated part of my experience. But I can also respond to the fact of aging with free *consent*. I can consent to the inevitability of aging and eventual death and then attempt to maximize possibilities open to me within this inevitability (9).

Closely related to freedom's choices of denial or consent are the choices between *care* and *self-preoccupation*. The anxiety I feel about my self-diminishment can motivate me to express concern almost completely toward myself. I can become preoccupied with maintaining myself and express interest in my world only insofar as it is necessary for the maintenance of myself. Or, on the other hand, I can express my concern over my self-diminishment by trying to care for both myself *and* my world. But here I run into difficulty. My self-in-the-world situation is diminishing; therefore, I cannot maintain it unless I try to renew it. But even here I run into further difficulty. I can renew and enrich my interests, my relationships, my vocational commitments, but I cannot renew in any lasting way my declining body. Even my interests will some day narrow when the energy to sustain them runs low and when I finally die. Therefore, the only part of my self-world reality that will permanently yield to maintenance and renewal is my world. The closest I can come to permanent self-maintenance and renewal is through the care and renewal of my *world*.

Phenomenological description does not itself reveal the status of my concern. It reveals only that I have an ambiguous concern for both myself and my world. Is my potential concern for the world a deep-seated desire to be useful and to make a contribution to something that will endure beyond myself? Is it an expression of my narcissistic affection for worldly extensions of myself? Is it a response to the call of God to serve the world? Does it reveal a dimension of ultimacy within my experience—a lure towards the unconditioned? Phenomenological description itself does not contain an answer to these questions. We must move beyond our direct experience and search for second order interpretations that will order and amplify the rudimentary meanings which description has revealed.

Scientific Perspectives on Aging

In an effort to open up our common experience of aging I have worked primarily at the level of phenomenological description, with brief mention of scientific knowledge about aging as diagnostic of the concrete experience of growing old. Let us now turn more directly to scientific perspectives on aging in order to gain insight into the depth of the ambiguity of our concern over aging—that concern which can express itself in care or self-preoccupation.

The work of Erik Erikson is an example of a species of social-scientific thinking on aging. Erikson's psychology mixes a loose form of phenomenological description with an evolutionary-adaptive explanation of human life, both at the level of the individual and the wider human species. His psychology is an example of an emerging style of social science—a style that combines with varying degrees of precision and self-consciousness existential-phenomenological description with adaptive-functional explanation. This style of social science is especially visible on the topic of aging because of the obvious importance of the perception of temporality in the situation of the person growing old. An example of this can be found in the highly significant work of Bernice Neugarten, who has incorporated Mannheim's concept of temporality into her understanding of the relevance of social and historical time to the phenomenon of aging (10).

The category of temporality is discussed throughout Erikson's psychology. With regard to the adult stage of life, Erikson gives fleeting but insightful phenomenological descriptions of man's sense of the meaning of the passing of time. It gives man a heightened sense that the past cannot be altered and that the future is more limited in its possibilities. These descriptions are assumed throughout the heart of Erikson's contribution to a psychology of aging developed in his discussion of the last two of his famous eight stages of life, the adult stages of generativity versus stagnation and the final stage of integrity versus despair (11). With these unsystematic but important phenomenological descriptions, Erikson fuses certain scientific models taken over from biology, ecology, and evolutionary theory. The most important of these models is the concept of epigenesis, which Erikson borrows from the biologist C. H. Stockard (12). Erikson's famous definition of epigenesis is as follows: "that everything that grows has a ground plan and out of this ground plan the parts arise, each part having its time of special ascendancy, until all parts have arisen to form a functioning whole" (13). This concept applies primarily to ego development and serves, in the thought of Erikson, to shift the basic logic of psychoanalysis greatly. The concept of epigenesis implies that environmental influences have a role in activating preexisting biological potentials; this is true for all the stages of development, including the crucial adult stage of generativity versus stagnation.

Erikson defines generativity as "the concern for establishing and guiding the next generation" (14). The concept is not necessarily limited to the literal procreation of children. Generativity refers to the creation and maintenance of a wide range of institutional and cultural resources necessary to guarantee the strength of present and succeeding generations. Erikson believes that individuals who fail to achieve the delicate synthesis that generativity entails become "stagnated" and express a narcissistic type of concern for themselves as though they were "their own . . . one and only child" (15). Erikson seems to be positing two tendencies in the human personality at the adult stage of development—one toward generativity and the other toward stagnation and self-concern. When generativity overcomes stagnation, Erikson believes that there emerges the virtue of *care*. Care, according to Erikson, "is the widening concern for what has been generated by love, necessity, or accident" (16).

What is often overlooked by Erikson's psychoanalytic colleagues is that Erikson is positing—in accordance with the logic of the epigenetic principle—instinctive foundations to generativity and care, foundations, however, that need to be activated by powerful symbols and favorable environments. For Erikson, generativity and care fulfill certain adaptive functions necessary for the evolutionary strength of the human cycle of generations. In one place he writes, "Evolution has made man a teaching as well as a learning animal, for dependency and maturity are reciprocal: mature man *needs to be needed*, and maturity is guided by the nature of that which must be cared for" (17). In another place Erikson writes that "man needs to teach" and that he has a "teaching passion." Or again, "Care is a quality essential for psychosocial evolution, for we are the teaching species." And finally, "Once we have grasped this interlocking of the human life stages, we understand that adult man is so constituted as to need to be needed" (18).

Time does not permit me to discuss how the adult stage of generativity and care are dependent upon and in fact guided by the earlier stages of human development. Let me simply emphasize that, for Erikson, aging during the middle years is a time when the human being has a strong need (indeed, proclivity if environment and ideology

are supportive) to expand his ego interests to become a "generator of
institutions" that can constitute appropriate "average expectable environments" for succeeding generations. If some success can be won
in this enterprise during the middle years, then later periods of aging
can be a time of *integrity*. Integrity is an "acceptance of one's one
and only life cycle" with no basic regret that it should have been otherwise; it also involves a "detached yet active concern with life" in
spite of declining vitality and approaching death (19). The presupposition of integrity is a prior attitude of generativity; it makes it possible for a person to live with what he has been and what he has brought
into this world that is likely to survive him.

There are rough parallels between our earlier phenomenological
description and Erikson's rather unsystematic combination of phe-
nomenological-descriptive and adaptive-explanatory points of view.
One of the main differences has to do with Erikson's handling of the
concept of care. In addition to describing care as a process of renew-
ing and maintaining the world, he posits instinctual foundations to
care and suggests that in caring man not only makes a contribution
to his world but promotes an intrinsic satisfaction within himself.
Hence, Erikson's coupling of the concepts of generativity and care
with his epigenetic theory of development gives us a type of "diagnostic" to the depths of the concept of care that we arrived at earlier
solely by the route of phenomenological description. At best, however, Erikson's understanding of the epigenetic foundations of care is
a scientific hypothesis—a scientific hunch—that man viewed entirely
from an adaptive-evolutionary point of view was destined to generativity and care if commanding ideals, environmental supports, and individual decision collaborate (20).

Erikson's contribution to a psychology of adulthood and aging
constitutes a new paradigm within psychoanalysis for an understanding of man. In addition to my own work in *Generative Man*, I have
noted similar recognition of this fact in the work of Daniel Yankelovich and William Barrett in *Ego and Instinct* (21) and in all the work
of Robert Lifton, especially in a recent article entitled "On Death
and the Continuity of Life: a 'New' Paradigm" (22). Lifton posits a
need within man for a sense of continuity with life (the larger species
and succeeding generations), which we try to work out through various forms of symbolic immortality. Death is as much a threat to this
need for continuity with the wider forms of life as it is a threat to
one's own individual existence (23).

This model of personality is implicit in a great deal of the psychological and sociological literature on aging. Much of this literature

emphasizes continuing needs on the part of people throughout the last half of the life span to be "useful" and to make a "contribution" even though this must necessarily take different forms in the later years of the life cycle. This literature acknowledges that the aging have needs for pleasure and relaxation and that these will be coupled with increasing disengagement from certain social and vocational responsibilities as life proceeds to its end. But this literature also recognizes another pervasive need that the aging and even the aged must satisfy—something close to what we have called generativity and care. A recent prominent textbook by Robert Butler and Myrna Lewis entitled *Aging and Mental Health* states it this way: "Human beings have a need to leave something of themselves behind when they die. This legacy may be children and grandchildren, work or art, personal possessions, memories, (etc.) . . . This legacy provides a sense of continuity, giving the older person a feeling of being able to participate even after death" (24).

Although aging may necessarily involve increasing degrees of disengagement, as Jung, William Henry, and Elaine Cumming have argued (25), others such as Erikson, Butler, Lewis, Lifton, and Neugarten would maintain that achieving a sense of continuity with the cycle of generations through care and appropriate forms of usefulness is a pervasive need of people throughout the aging years.

It has been the implication of our two perspectives on common experience, the phenomenological and the scientific, that there is some thrust toward permanency and the unconditioned in our experience of aging—some *telos* to transcend the limits of one's finite life and gain a significance that surpasses the boundaries of our individual life cycles. To amplify the grounds of this rudimentary drive toward what Lifton calls symbolic immortality, we must turn to historic religious symbols and to metaphysics. Among possible religious symbols, the symbols of "salvation" and "hope" may help us the most with our task of developing a theology of aging.

Aging, Salvation, and Hope

My task is to determine now what correlation can be made between common experience as we have analyzed it and biblical symbols, legends, and stories. Since throughout this paper our emphasis has been on method, I must stress that I turn to biblical myth and symbol not with the conviction that it is here only that truth can be found. Rather, I turn to this source out of the conviction that a fuller, more encompassing vision can be found in religious language, a vision that

may suggest a more embracing truth, amplifying some of the meanings and answering some of the questions revealed in our analysis of
common experience. For our analysis of common experience revealed
that implicit to the experience of aging is a thrust toward transcending one's individual life through care. Yet neither phenomenology
nor the adaptive-evolutionary perspective can state the grounds upon
which this *telos* can be affirmed as a possibility. Upon what ground
can I believe that my care will have lasting significance?

William Beardslee's work on the meaning of "hope" and James
Lapsley's contributions on the meaning of "salvation" should prove
helpful (26). From the perspective of these men, the oldest oral rec-
ords about Jesus are apocalyptic narratives or stories that project a
distinctive vision of the relationship between the present and the future. God's rule over the world—the Kingdom of God—was destined
to come at some undisclosed moment in the future. But already in
the present, this Kingdom was beginning to manifest itself, and Jesus,
his ministry, and his healings are signs of the coming of the Kingdom.
Both Lapsley and Beardslee point out that those who have faith in
the coming of the Kingdom are expected to participate in God's sal-
vatory activity of ushering in the Kingdom. Not a passive but an active hope is the response of the early Christian to the dawning but
not yet fully realized Kingdom of God. Beardslee believes that the
motifs of participation and reward are to be found in each of the
three most fundamental sources for the faith of primitive Christianity—Q, Mark, and Paul. With regard to the motif of participation,
Beardslee writes this about the ancient oral tradition of Q: "God is
doing a work. It is God's work, and men cannot force it, but the community is called into the same task as its Lord" (27). Certain parabol-
ic expressions serve to illustrate this. "The harvest is plentiful, but
the laborers are few; pray therefore the Lord of the harvest to send
out laborers into his harvest" (Luke 10:3). The motif of participation
can be found in the tremendous emphasis upon apostolic vocation to
be found in Mark and the writings of Paul (28).

Beardslee believes that the motifs of participation and reward reinforce one another. He writes: "The reward motif and the participation motif reinforce each other in expressing a stance in which it is
self-evident that beyond the negation of self there lies a new life in
which one already participates, and in which one's goal-directed strivings are not just self-projection, but are part of the process of God's
work, and hence take on real significance for the future, being taken
up into the eschatological consummation" (29). The negation that
Beardslee is referring to is the negation of both sacrificial participa-

tion and death. The participation of early Christians, both individually and corporately, in God's saving and redeeming work gave them a
sense that their own finite efforts were caught up in the activity of
God and therefore had an objective significance to them that would
transcend their own suffering and eventual death.

In conjunction with this understanding of participation and reward, Beardslee develops a unique interpretation of the apocalyptic
symbolism of the "end." Beardslee denies that Jewish and Christian
apocalyptic views of the end can be understood as total destruction.
He writes: "Despite all the symbolism of destruction that has been
taken up into our modern imagination from traditional apocalyptic,
this ancient Jewish Christian form of faith was full of hope. Beyond
the destruction it saw a new creation" (30). In addition, symbolism
of the end cannot be understood as an undifferentiated unification
of all things with God. Beardslee states it as follows:

> Most New Testament symbolism, and most apocalyptic symbolism general-
> ly, does not point toward a "total end." . . . the "end" is typically con-
> ceived as the end of a stage. . . . One factor that held in check the thrust to-
> ward a total end—a total loss of differentiation—was the conviction that
> God took differentiated concrete existence so seriously that he would, in
> one way or another, take it up into the final fulfillment. (31)

Hence, differentiated finite existence through participation in God's
saving activity is somehow taken up and preserved in the life of God.
This comes very close to Lapsley's reading of the meaning of salvation. He writes: "Salvation . . . must refer primarily to the preservation in the life of God of the values realized in the world, especially
in the lives of men" (32).

What does this understanding of hope and salvation in these crucial
New Testament sources suggest for the problem of aging? Our two
perspectives on the common experience of aging revealed that there
is within it a thrust toward transcending through care the limitations
of one's individual life. There is also within the experience of aging
the temptation to sink back into self-preoccupation and stagnation.
New Testament apocalypticism is a symbolic representation of an objective activity on the part of God that transforms the world and preserves the values of those who participate in His work. New Testament apocalypticism gives ideological reinforcement to our efforts to
make generativity and care victorious over stagnation and self-absorption. It furthermore conveys the idea that efforts to care for and renew the world are not totally dependent upon my own individual efforts. Therefore, when our own vitality declines and the range of our

contributions becomes narrowed, we can still have the sense that our efforts will have some objective meaning in the life of God and that activity toward the renewal of the world will go on beyond the cessation of our own labors.

Metaphysical Foundations to the New Testament Vision

As I have indicated, the purpose of this article is to illustrate a method on an issue in practical theology. Time does not permit me to elaborate in detail any of the steps I have taken. I want to contend, however, that we cannot claim truth for the apocalyptic vision of Q and Mark without asking if this vision can be articulated in terms of a metaphysics that can be argued before the court of rational discourse. In the context of this paper, I must limit myself to making reference to certain enterprises where this question is being pursued. Once again, I will turn to the work of William Beardslee, who in turn makes use of the process metaphysics of A. N. Whitehead and Charles Hartshorne.

Process metaphysics should be understood as a metaphysical extension of the view of the world associated with the post-Darwinist evolutionary-adaptive perspective on life. We confronted the evolutionary-adaptive point of view in the work of Erik Erikson. In fact, most of the social sciences, and for that matter most of the sciences of man dealing with aging, are roughly evolutionary-adaptive in their philosophical orientation. Although many of these disciplines are narrowly behavioristic and functional with regard to their Darwinism, others are more emergent-evolutionary in the fashion of Whitehead. Erikson himself has an emergent-evolutionary context of meanings to his psychology. Barrett and Yankelovich note this when they write that Erikson's concept of epigenesis has "similarities to Whitehead's concept of organism as an emergent structure" (33). Hence, Whiteheadian philosophy may be a fortuitous perspective from which to discern the metaphysical foundations of generativity and care.

Beardslee himself is interested in discovering the metaphysical foundations of care, very much in the way Erikson defines it. His point of entry is through the idea of the infinite. He repudiates the presently popular resuscitation of the ancient concept of the undifferentiated-indefinite infinite, which he believes has reemerged in the writings of Emerson, Alan Watts, Aldous Huxley, Norman Brown, Richard Rubenstein, and Thomas Altizer. Instead, he develops the idea of the definite infinite and uses the thinking of Whitehead to amplify its meaning. Beardslee reminds us of the distinction in Whitehead's thought between the primordial and the consequent nature of God (34). Although both of these dimensions of God are abstractions from God's concrete nature, the primordial nature refers to God's eternal envisagement of all eternal objects or possibilities; it is this dimension of God that comes closer to the ancient idea of indefinite infinite or totality. The other dimension of God, the consequent nature, is infinite by virtue of its unlimited capacity to integrate into the life of God the actual values that emerge from other actual events and people. We need not labor here the details of this distinction and the various justifications for it put forth by Whitehead. We need only to be reminded that it is in the interplay between God's primordial nature and his consequent nature that care becomes a possibility. God provides each actual entity with an appropriate possibility for that entity's initial aim or *telos*. But the actual values which that entity "chooses" and passes on to subsequent actual occasions are also taken up and preserved in the consequent nature of God. In this view, all entities (and certainly more complex societies such as human beings) through the values that they choose make contributions, for good or ill, not only to their successors but also to the very experience of God. Hence, process metaphysics gives man a house for his hope and a house for his care. It reveals to us in the context of our aging a metaphysical vision whereby our efforts to care for and renew our world not only are communicated causally to succeeding generations but actually also are saved from perishing by God Himself. In this view of things, time is taken as real and the infinity of God is concrete; it offers a metaphysical vision capable of conceptualizing and sustaining the religious experience of Judaism and Christianity. As Beardslee writes, this tradition "introduced into the West an understanding of infinity as not simply indefinite but as a concrete infinity of valued qualities" (35).

The Contemporary Sociocultural Context of Aging

The last step in my effort to develop a practical theology of aging must now be taken. To take this last step I want to set aside the important question of what specific programs the church should have in order to minister to the aging. Rather, I want to ask what critical leverage on contemporary society does this theology of aging suggest? In addition, what programmatic consequences would follow from the above analysis?

Social science research into the situation of the aging in contemporary Western society points to the possible development of a potentially disastrous state of affairs. Both phenomenological and scientific perspectives on aging revealed a major existential conflict between care (or generativity) and stagnation or self-preoccupation. There are strong forces in contemporary Western society that tend to aggravate this conflict and to reinforce the retreat into stagnation and self-absorption. This is to say that several trends in Western society are working to frustrate the thrust toward care in aging people.

What are these forces? There seem to be three—earlier retirement, longer periods of healthy life after retirement, and growing isolation of the aging from the rest of society and the cycle of the generations. The spread of automation and the likelihood of decreasing rates of economic growth suggest that the trends toward early retirement will accelerate. Expressing care and generativity through one's formal vocation will be a time-limited experience for millions of people in the future society. On the other hand, our highly differentiated and mobile society plus the dominance of the nuclear family have led to an increasing isolation of the aging and the aged from the rest of society. In the future, this can begin happening to people in their early fifties and continue over a period of forty or fifty years. We have not even begun to think of alternatives to formal vocation for the healthy aging to express their needs for generativity and care. Therefore, in a variety of ways, Western society may increasingly limit the freedom and possibility for the aging to make meaningful and age-appropriate contributions to either the larger society or to the life and memory of God. It follows from this that the theology developed here would favor programs that would undergird the basic health and livelihood of the aging, that would find appropriate alternatives to formal vocations for the expression of care, and that would break down the isolation of the aging and aged from the total cycle of the generations.

To come up with programs accomplishing these goals, certain value commitments in Western society may have to change. Values connected with the idea of care will have to replace values connected with economic utility and aimless leisure. We must challenge both the idea that a person is only of worth or contributing when he is gainfully employed and the idea that the last stages of life should be a time of irrelevant comfort and preadolescent indulgence. Although it may be true that the aging want and need larger doses of relaxation and disengagement, they also want to express care for the cycle of the generations and the future of the world.

References

1. Maurice Merleau-Ponty, *The Primacy of Perception and Other Essays* (Evanston: Northwestern University Press, 1964), pp. 64-78.

2. Ibid., p. 67.
3. Paul Ricoeur, *Freedom and Nature* (Evanston: Northwestern University Press, 1966), p. 87.
4. Ibid., p. 88.
5. The method of correlation I have in mind here should not be confused with Tillich's method of correlating answers from revelation with questions from existence. Although the method I am discussing includes that method, it goes beyond this. It is closer to the method of correlation described throughout the works of Seward Hiltner, Daniel Day Williams, and, most recently, David Tracy. See Chapter 6 of my *Atonement and Psychotherapy* (Philadelphia: Westminster Press, 1966), pp. 149-72; and David Tracy, "The Task of Fundamental Theology," *Journal of Religion* 54, no. 1 (January 1974):18.
6. For an important discussion of how theoretically true statements are not always directly relevant for creative adaptation, see Heinz Hartmann, *Ego Psychology and the Problem of Adaptation* (New York: International Universities Press, 1958), p. 19.
7. See Simone de Beauvoir's summary of the physiology of aging, *The Coming of Age* (New York: Warner Publications, 1973), pp. 27-56.
8. This emphasis upon the mediated nature of the experience of aging and eventual death is compatible with the point of view developed by Paul Ricoeur in *Freedom and Nature*, pp. 432-33 and 456-63.
9. My analysis of denial and consent is closely parallel to Ricoeur's description of refusal and consent, *Freedom and Nature*, pp. 463-80.
10. Bernice Neugarten and Nancy Datn, "Sociological Perspectives on the Life Cycle," in *Life-Span Developmental Psychology*, ed. Paul Baltes and Warner Schaire (New York: Academic Press, 1973), pp. 53-71.
11. Discussions of these last stages of life appear in several different places in Erik H. Erikson's writings, notably in *Childhood and Society*, 2nd ed. (New York: W. W. Norton & Co., 1963), pp. 247-74; *Identity and the Life Cycle* (New York: International Universities Press, 1959), pp. 50-100; and *Youth: Identity and Crisis* (New York: W. W. Norton & Co., 1968), pp. 91-141.
12. Erikson, *Childhood and Society*, p. 65.
13. Erikson, *Youth: Identity and Crisis*, p. 92.
14. Ibid., p. 138.
15. Erikson, *Childhood and Society*, p. 267; and *Youth: Identity and Crisis*, p. 138.
16. Erik H. Erikson, *Insight and Responsibility* (New York: W. W. Norton & Co., 1964), p. 130.
17. Erikson, *Youth: Identity and Crisis*, p. 138 (italics mine).
18. Erikson, *Insight and Responsibility*, p. 130.
19. Erikson, *Youth: Identity and Crisis*, p. 140.
20. Recent work on the theory of instinct advances the idea that there is no way arbitrarily to separate instinct from learning. See William Barrett and Daniel Yankelovich, *Ego and Instinct* (New York: Random House, 1970), pp. 347-82 and 441-46. Therefore, these authors assume that all instinctive tendencies, especially in man, need an "average expectable environment" or a "continuum of experience" to activate and stabilize these tendencies. Furthermore, they argue that man's ethical tendencies—even his altruistic care for his own children and for the wider human race—have instinctive foundations, but foundations that must have both environmental and ideological supports in order to become manifest. Explicit in their work and implicit in the work of Erikson is a repudiation in the field of ethics of the entire Kantian tradition of the separation of nature from freedom, history, and the realm of moral action.
21. Barrett and Yankelovich, *Ego and Instinct*.

22. Robert Lifton, "On Death and the Continuity of Life: A 'New' Paradigm," *History of Childhood Quarterly* 1, no. 4 (Spring 1974): 681-96.
23. Freud posited in his later theory beginning with *Beyond the Pleasure Principle* (1920) an unconscious need for union, which is similar to what Erikson is speaking about under the rubric of generativity and Lifton with the idea of symbolic immortality. The difference is that Freud never disentangled his later concept of Eros from his earlier Helmholtzian model of sexual energies. In addition, in Erikson and Lifton, generativity and symbolic immortality take on a considerably different valuation tone, are more directly associated with the central organizing processes of the ego, and are actively invoked as major interpretative concepts in their psychologies.
24. Robert Butler and Myrna Lewis, *Aging and Mental Health* (St. Louis: C. V. Mosby Co., 1973), p. 23.
25. Elaine Cumming and William Henry, *Growing Old: The Process of Disengagement* (New York: Basic Books, 1966). For critiques of the disengagement theory of aging see Bernice Neugarten et al., "Personality and Patterns of Aging," and Arnold M. Rose, "A Current Theoretical Issue in Social Gerontology," in *Middle Age and Aging*, ed. Bernice Neugarten (Chicago: University of Chicago Press, 1968).
26. James N. Lapsley, *Salvation and Health* (Philadelphia: Westminster Press, 1972); and William Beardslee, *A House for Hope* (Philadelphia: Westminster Press, 1972).
27. Beardslee, *House for Hope*, p. 120.
28. Ibid., pp. 120 and 124.
29. Ibid., pp. 120-21.
30. Ibid, p. 98.
31. Ibid., pp. 101-102.
32. Lapsley, *Salvation and Health*, p. 53.
33. Barrett and Yankelovich, *Ego and Instinct*, p. 150.
34. Beardslee, *House for Hope*, p. 68. For Whitehead's basic discussions of his understanding of God see his *Religion in the Making* (New York: Meridian Press, 1960), pp. 66-80, 91-109, 143-50; *Process and Reality* (New York: Harper & Row, 1960), pp. 46-52, 519-33; *Science and the Modern World* (New York: Mentor Books, 1956), pp. 173-80.
35. Beardslee, *House for Hope*, p. 71.

Discussion and Comment

Seward Hiltner, Ph.D.

There were two types of discussion at the workshop: in plenary sessions following each address, and in five small groups consisting of seven or eight members each. Both kinds of discussion were tape recorded. The budget had not permitted an audio expert; and when an effort was made to produce transcriptions from the tapes, they turned out to offer various degrees of difficulty in being understood. When it became evident that no single discussion could be transcribed clearly, William C. McMorran spent long hours listening to tapes and reading transcriptions, attempting to note key points of discussion in all groups, since the line followed in any one group could not clearly be traced. Working from McMorran's notes, and from some transcriptions, I note below what appear to be focal points arising in discussions by one or more of the groups—with no guarantee possible that other equally important points may not be inadvertently lost in this summation. The points are presented in a roughly logical order that does not necessarily correspond to their sequence in the discussions.

Propaedeutic to Theology

In nearly all the small groups, perhaps in spite of the fact that all the members were experienced discussants, some members found it necessary to begin with a personal experience, usually brief and with few details, about aging or older people in their own families or in those of friends. In some groups such stories appeared later as well. It would seem that, even to a sophisticated group, aging is still "emotionally loaded," so that a kind of existential transition had to be made between the more or less objective facts and the consideration of theological approaches.

After the "stories," some of the small groups moved at once into theological issues, while others dealt initially with other than uniquely theological perspectives. I shall deal next with these "other perspective" matters that appeared in the discussion of several groups. It was clear that no one thought a theology of aging possible without taking into account other approaches as well.

1. *Knowledge about aging.* Considerable (and in my judgment, appropriate) emphasis was placed on the limitations on our knowledge of aging from almost every relevant perspective. One group especially noted that theologians are more likely to be sensitive to social and value approaches and may therefore take too lightly what the biological, chemical, and related approaches can contribute. No group failed to say in some way that multidisciplinary studies of aging are basic, that a theology of aging cannot be done without them, and that theologians need to guard against their own biases on what they do and do not regard as important.

2. *Aging and identity crises.* None of the groups forgot that understanding aging is more than understanding people in later years. Granted that the movement into older years may usually be accompanied by or perceived as an identity crisis, several groups noted that in the normal lifetime there are likely to be several identity crises over aging, and that the timing of these may be unpredictable, so that relatively early education about aging (perhaps above all making the topic both serious and tolerable) is important to help when these crises come.

3. *Aging and disparities.* Although it was emphasized by some groups more than others, all acknowledged to some degree the impossibility of making any general statements about people in the aging process without genuine attention to the disparities according to income, to racial and cultural differences, and to being male or female. On the average, for instance, blacks die several years earlier than whites in the United States. Poor people experience older years and earlier aging phases very differently from persons in either middle-class or upper-class positions. Women live longer on the average than men and, sometimes partly because of this fact, experience aging at various stages differently from them. No "homogenizing" of all such experiences can be permitted if a relevant theology of aging is to result. One group felt that it was essential to "listen to the oppressed" in relation to aging and older people, as in other areas of significant social concern.

4. *Aging and the extended family.* Although no one believed that the older form of the extended family could be brought back, more than one group explored what might be called its "equivalents." The discussions were attitudinal rather than structural or programmatic. With people living longer and in better health, older families have the

potentiality of emancipation from the rigidities of the "nuclear family" pattern. They might therefore take the lead in crossing the lines
between generations so that eventually all ages could relate more free-
ly to one another. A movement in that direction, it was held, would
be toward the equivalency of the extended family.

5. *Ambivalent attitudes toward aging.* Even slightly rose colored
views, and even dimly dismal outlooks, were checked in the group
discussions by the acknowledgment that society holds ambivalent,
and indeed often conflicting, attitudes both toward aging and older
people. On the one hand, there are the ignorings or "put-downs" of
older people; and, in reaction, there are the temptations to "glamor-
ize." It was agreed that neither attitude is justified or helpful and that
exposure of one-sided stances is useful, as is the recognition that all
of us tend to be drawn into the generally ambivalent position of our
culture.

Issues in a Theology of Aging

The small groups differed in the proportion of time they devoted
to the issues listed above and the more clearly theological ones below.
No group, however, failed to spend some time on both.

Since the formal addresses of the workshop were provocative, of
course small groups gave them some attention in their discussions. No
group assumed the task of careful critique of any or all papers presented. There were expressions both of agreement and disagreement
about particular points speakers had made or failed to make. Most
comment about the addresses was tucked by each discussant into
whatever point he was attempting to make.

It is fielder's choice as to how, in retrospect, the small group discussions about a theology of aging might be organized. Were someone to go through the materials as I have, he might well emerge with
different categories than those that follow. Nevertheless, my effort is
to report rather than editorialize.

Hope (Finitude and Potentiality)

Discussion of hope appeared to some degree in all the groups. No
group took time to analyze the concept, but all seemed to assume
such factors as: where there is simple expectation, hope is not needed; hope is needed only in the face of difficulties that might bring
despair; and genuine hope is neither denial nor merely compensatory.
Some groups discussed death not simply as an event but as a present

psychic experience. They were inclined to suggest that a realistic confrontation of death in both senses (as in Judaism and Christianity)
combined with the faith that somehow (the way not known to us)
death is not the "end" is the most basic difficulty that genuine hope
has to confront.

One group believed that older people may be the "precursors" for
the kind of attitude toward aging that is needed by persons at all
stages of life, for they may have confronted our human finitude more
directly than most of us. If at the same time they have discovered the
potentiality still present, waiting only for them to actualize it, then
such older people may teach us all. A related idea from a group was
that, for at least some older people, there may be new opportunities
for "self-giving." If the "venture in self-giving" is something our culture tends to discourage (Don't be a sucker), then here also some older persons can be guides for all.

One group saw in older years (for those persons not penalized on
economic, racial, or similar grounds) the possibility for a "second
childhood," which, far from being regressive, can be a form of "new
birth" in the sense of the New Testament. The phrase used by this
group was the potential for "play and exploration." While not considering that angle, another group suggested reexamination of the Bible, especially the New Testament, for its apocalyptic message in the
light of what we are now beginning to see about aging. One or two
points in David Tracy's address were regarded as possible starters for
such consideration.

Possible Paradigms of Aging

Perhaps "paradigms" suggests something deeper than any discussion group could grapple for in two or three sessions. But there was a
groping for analogies, or even models, that could highlight the theological understanding of aging as a process. One such suggestion concerned the "trajectory" of aging, which ought not to be ruled out because it comes from baseballs or bullets. I believe (although the tran-
scripts are not clear) that the intent of the trajectory analogy was not
to show that life begins low, rises to an apex, and then drops down.
It was rather to show the speed or energy at all points along the way,
and the immensely greater horizontal than vertical distances involved.
Alone, it may be insufficient to lead to a paradigm, for it could slide
back into the model that Paul W. Pruyser explicitly rejected in his address. Nevertheless, whether that is the analogy to pursue, or some
other, several groups at least began a search for paradigms.

One group used two different language styles in speaking of the "confrontation of finitude" along with a "grab for grace" (the latter of which was attributed to John Wesley). Yet if these dialectical concepts were analyzed further in relation to aging, it is possible that a paradigm might emerge from them—even if non-Methodists are less honest than Wesley in admitting the impulse to grab.

A third candidate for guide toward paradigm appeared in one group as a discussion of scarcity and abundance. Not excluding economic and similar matters, that discussion suggested that attitudes toward aging are still dominated by "scarcity" connotations in a broad sense, and that this is misleading in the realm of the spirit and, increasingly, in other realms as well. Perhaps the paradigm(s) that may eventually prove most accurate and relevant will grow out of other notions than those mentioned above. But these may be starts in the right direction.

Aging and Vocation

The group giving most attention to this topic suggested that there should remain a dialectic (or tension) between vocation as productive work (in the ordinary sense) and vocation as serious focused energy investment—rather than a fusion of the two ideas. This would encourage those even at older ages to understand appropriate energy investments as part of their vocation or calling from God; and yet it would not deny that some people have to engage in productive work if basic needs of all are to be met.

One group considered what was called "youth idolatry," suggesting the preference of the culture for the unlined feature, the situation where irrevocable choices are yet to be made, and the high value placed on what might be called "speedy vitality." Going along with that in fact, it was declared, is often a tendency to put older people on a pedestal, or at least to appear to do so. Both attitudes were held to be distortions. The first was called idolatry because its conception of vitality may indeed almost be an ultimate object of desire and commitment. The second tends to be compensatory, even hypocritical; so its idolatrous character lies not in genuineness but in its spurious attempt to show respect where genuine respect is absent.

Only one group discussed possible "decisions to die," and the analysis of what that phrase suggests was barely begun. But the context of the brief discussion is worth considering in terms of the context in which it appeared, namely, that of vocation. Whether the decision to die is dramatic, or simply letting go the denial pattern, it could conceivably be a part of a person's truly hearing the calling of God to him or her. That could help, at all stages of life and not solely older years, to see a dimension of vocation that has usually remained unstated.

The Family of God

One group especially took the family (or household) of God metaphor of the Bible and suggested that recapturing its biblical intent, but putting into its concrete content the whole range of ages we now know, could be of great value not only for the traditional purpose (as a model of the church) but also as a theological statement for all mankind in a heterogeneous society. The group was not combatting the "family of man" idea. It was, instead, trying to show that that valuable secular idea could have a theological counterpart, which could be no less universal in its goals because it comes from particular perspectives, and which may have a firmer rootage because it does not rest wholly upon mankind's love or creative powers. The further suggestion was that, with more people living longer and with at least more potential for creativity, the age span of the family of God must be considered in a new light. Beyond that, of course, the family of God may become the communion of saints (when saints means only on the way and not yet or ever arrived) in which common createdness under God and common humanity are shared not only with all ages but with all ancestors and descendants.

Concluding Comment

In addition to rewriting the first article on "Facts and Needs" and writing the present one summarizing salient points in the discussions, I have also reread carefully and done technical editing on the other four articles that were presented to the workshop as addresses. I find that my sense of the importance of the subject has grown with this work rather than diminished. No one of the writers here suggests that we have arrived at a theology of aging, whatever its content. Indeed, it may be that our writers, as a group, have been overly cautious rather than otherwise. I suspect that each of them has ideas about next steps toward a theology of aging that he did not include here. Nevertheless, with a topic as significant as this, better that claims be modest.

It is my hope that, collectively, the articles coming out of the workshop may perform two kinds of functions. First and most obvious, they should stimulate more work, reflection, research, and writing on a theology of aging and, concomitantly, more teaching about it (and the other kinds of knowledge needed along with theology) for clergy, theological students, and church people generally. Second, since our society is slowly beginning to recognize that it has paid far too little attention to aging, I hope that this report will suggest to many who have such a concern, no matter what their religion, if any, that the kind of theological approaches begun in this book have a significant place in any comprehensive consideration of aging. Although my colleagues may have made only a start, the quality of their reflections is such that I think they will stimulate others to pursue the intriguing paths they have begun to cut. I hope they will also discourage those looking only for gimmicks.

Even if this report does nothing else than make its reader, from now on, say, "Aging? That's me!" at whatever stage of life he or she is, it will have gone a long distance. If, in addition, both churchmen and atheists say, "Perhaps theology has something to contribute to society about aging," then we will have succeeded in our task at this stage.

APPENDIX

Workshop Participants:
Conference on the Theology of Aging

James B. Ashbrook, Ph.D., Professor of Psychology and Theology, Colgate Rochester/Bexley Hall/Crozer Center, Rochester, New York. He is an ordained American Baptist minister.

Arthur H. Becker, Ph.D., Professor of Pastoral Care and Social Ethics, Lutheran Theological Seminary, Columbus, Ohio. He is an ordained minister of the American Lutheran Church.

William C. Bier, S.J., Ph.D., Associate Vice President–Academic Affairs, Fordham University, New York. He is a Roman Catholic priest.

Richard A. Bollinger, M. Div., Director, Division of Religion and Psychiatry, The Menninger Foundation, Topeka, Kansas. He is an ordained minister of the Church of the Brethren.

C. W. Brister, Ph.D., Professor of Pastoral Ministry, Southwestern Baptist Theological Seminary, Fort Worth, Texas. He is an ordained Southern Baptist minister.

Richard E. Cleary, O.S.F.S., M.A., Director of Field Education, De Sales Hall School of Theology, Hyattsville, Maryland. He is a Roman Catholic priest.

William M. Clements, Ph.D., Associate Chaplain, Area Director of Pastoral Counseling, the Baptist Medical Centers, Birmingham, Alabama. He is an ordained minister of the United Methodist Church.

Lowell G. Colston, Ph.D., Professor of Pastoral Care, Christian Theological Seminary, Indianapolis, Indiana. He is an ordained minister of the Christian Church.

Douglas A. Dahlquist, Ph.D., Associate Professor of Pastoral Care, Bethel Theological Seminary, St. Paul, Minnesota. He is an ordained minister of the Baptist General Conference.

Harry DeWire, Ph.D., Professor of Pastoral Theology and Psychology, United Theological Seminary, Dayton, Ohio. He is an ordained minister of the United Methodist Church.

Thomas E. Droege, Ph.D., Professor at Valparaiso University, Valparaiso, Indiana. He is an ordained minister of the Lutheran Church Missouri Synod.

Mary Alice Douty Edwards, Ed.D., Professor of Christian Education, Wesley Theological Seminary, Washington, D.C. She is a member of the United Methodist Church.

Alan Pembroke Farr, S.T.M., Research Fellow, Pacific School of Religion, Berkeley, California. He is an ordained minister of the United Church of Christ.

Robert T. Huber, M.A., Director of Special Educational Program Development, Institute of Gerontology, The University of Michigan, Ann Arbor, Michigan. He is an ordained minister of the Christian Church.

Homer L. Jernigan, Ph.D., Albert V. Danielson Professor of Pastoral Care and Counseling, Boston University School of Theology, Boston, Massachusetts. He is an ordained minister of the United Methodist Church.

Hugh A. Koops, Ph.D., Professor of Church and Community, New Brunswick
  Theological Seminary, New Brunswick, New Jersey. He is an ordained minis-
  ter of the Reformed Church of America.
Donald P. McNeill, C.S.C., Ph.D., Assistant Professor of Theology, University of
  Notre Dame, Notre Dame, Indiana. He is a Roman Catholic priest.
Daniel L. Migliore, Ph.D., Associate Professor of Theology, Princeton Theologi-
  cal Seminary, Princeton, New Jersey. He is an ordained minister of the Unit-
  ed Presbyterian Church.
Edgar A. Mills, Ph.D., Associate Professor of Sociology, St. John's University,
  Jamaica, New York. He is a member of the United Presbyterian Church.
Allen Moore, Ph.D., Professor of Religion and Personality and Education at the
  School of Theology at Claremont, Claremont, California. He is an ordained
  minister of the United Methodist Church.
Peter J. Naus, Ph.D., Assistant Professor of Psychology and Director of Studies
  in Family Life and Sex Education, St. Jerome's College, Waterloo, Ontario.
  He is a member of the Roman Catholic Church.
Paul Nicely, M.Div., Professor of Pastoral Care, Methodist Theological School,
  Delaware, Ohio. He is an ordained priest in the Episcopal Church.
Robert A. Preston, Ph.D., Professor of Pastoral Care, Lexington Theological Sem-
  inary, Lexington, Kentucky. He is an ordained minister of the Christian Church.
Thomas Pugh, Ph.D., Professor of Psychology of Religion and Pastoral Care, In-
  terdenominational Theological Center, Atlanta. He is an ordained minister.
J. Deotis Roberts, Ph.D., Dean, School of Theology, Virginia Union University,
  Richmond, Virginia. He is an ordained minister of the American Baptist
  Church.
William F. Rogers, Ph.D., Professor of Pastoral Care, Eden Theological Seminary,
  Webster Groves, Missouri. He is an ordained minister of the United Church of
  Christ.
Bobby Joe Saucer, Ph.D., Faculty member, Union Theological Seminary, New
  York. He is an ordained minister.
David Silverman, D.H.L., Faculty member, Jewish Theological Seminary, New
  York. He is a rabbi in the Conservative branch of Judaism.
John W. Stettner, Th.D., Professor of Pastoral Care, McCormick Theological
  Seminary, Chicago, Illinois. He is an ordained minister of the United Presby-
  terian Church.
Vernon L. Stremke, Ph.D., Professor of Pastoral Theology, Pacific Lutheran The-
  ological Seminary, Berkeley, California. He is an ordained minister of the Lu-
  theran Church of America.
Kenneth L. Vaux, Th.D., Director of Theology, Professor of Theology and Ethics, Institute of Religion & Human Development, Texas Medical Center, Hou-
  ston, Texas. He is an ordained minister of the United Presbyterian Church.

Representatives from the
National Retired Teachers Association and the
American Association of Retired Persons

Ann Fitzgerald, New Haven, Connecticut
Joseph A. Fitzgerald, New Haven, Connecticut
Earl N. Kragnes, Washington, D.C.
William C. McMorran, Washington, D.C.
Boris Steiman, Kansas City, Missouri
W. Randolph Thornton, Washington, D.C.
Douglas O. Woodruff, Salt Lake City, Utah

INDEX

Abandonment, sense of among older people, 111.

Abraham, concept of old age in, 136.

Activity version of iconic illusion, 103.

Aging: denial of, 97, 105; and eschatology, 119-34; evasion of, 97; as evoking concern, 155; experience of time in, 106; as expression of human authenticity, 124; as growth, 104; and hope, 160-63, 170-71; and the iconic illusion, 103; and identity crises, 169; knowledge of as limited, 135-36, 169; losses in, 107ff.; as maturing, 104-105; Mishnah view of, 139; and modalities of time, 131-33; and mortality, 98; paradigms of, 171-72; phenomenological responses to, 155; phenomenology of, 154-56; repression of, 97; and "sabbath" of life, 147-50; and social class, 143-47; and the vital balance, 105.

Aging process, problems in understanding, 105.

Agitation, in older people, 110.

Altizer, Thomas, 163.

Ambivalent attitudes toward older people, 101.

American Association of Retired Persons, 93, 95, 96.

Ancestor worship as cultural phenomenon, 104.

Andrus, Ethel Percy, 96.

Apocalyptic: in Jesus, 161-62; as model of meaning, 127ff.

Artistic version of iconic illusion, 103.

Ashbrook, James B., 175.

"Atomic moments," as view of time, 122-26.

Attitudes: toward older people in our society, 101, 107, 170; toward older people in different cultures,

104; toward older people by the Greeks, 104.

Augustine, the "three presents" of, 105.

Authenticity: aging as expression of, 124; in eschatology, 129-31.

Barrett, William, 159, 163.

Beardslee, William, 161, 162, 163.

Beauvoir, Simone de, 132, 145, 146.

Becker, Arthur H., 175.

Bier, William C., 175.

Blau, Zena Smith, 144, 145.

Bollinger, Richard A., 175.

Brain, in aging, 105.

Brister, C. W., 175.

Brown, Norman O., 128, 130, 163.

Browning, Don S., 128, 130, 151-67.

Bultmann, Rudolf, 127, 128.

Butler, Robert, 160.

Calvin, John, 129.

Campbell, Joseph, 140.

Care: Erikson's view of, 158; as response to recognition of aging, 156.

Children: experience of time by, 106; and older people, 115-16.

Christian symbols of temporality, 122.

Christian theology, meaning of today, 129-32.

Claudel, Paul, 146.

Cleary, Richard E., 175.

Clements, William M., 175.

Coles, Robert, 108, 114.

Colston, Lowell G., 175.

Coming of age, 104.

Concern evoked by recognition of aging, 155.

Correlation in theology, 120-21, 152.

Counter-Reformation, 129-30.

Credos by older people, 116.

Cumming, Elaine, 160.